AF595407

Are You Sure?

A Story of Aesthetic World

BHUSHAN KHAIRNAR

Rigi Publication
777, Street No. 9, Krishna Nagar
Khanna-141401
Punjab (India)
Email: info@rigipublication.com
Website: www.rigipublication.com

First published by Rigi Publication 2013

Copyright © Bhushan Khairnar 2013

All rights reserved

This is a work of fiction. Names, characters, places and incidents either are the product of the author's imagination or are used fictitiously , and any resemblance to any actual persons, living or dead, events or locales, is purely coincidental.

ISBN: 978-81-921311-2-2

Typeset by: Ram Sharma

Printed at KS Printing Press

This book is sold subject to the condition that it shall not by way of trade or otherwise, be lent, resold, hired out, circulated, and no reproduction in any form, in whole or in part (except for brief quotations in critical articles or reviews) may be made without written permission from the publishers.

Contents

PART FOUR

The Myth of Life

Acknowledgements

I am aware of having accumulated more debts of gratitude than I ever have before. I am genuinely grateful to all the people who have helped me.

I am particularly thankful to my friends, Amit Chauhan and Mahendra Waghmare for their constant support, guidance, time and genuine criticism.

I am also particularly grateful to Rahul Khairnar for developing prototype fonts and technical guidance. I am also thankful to Mehul Gajjar for the graphical support.

I am especially thankful to Rigi Publication team, especially, Umesh Sehgal, owner, for proper guidance and support.

I, most definitely, would not have been able to complete this work without the support of my wife, Khushbu, whose love and motivation has been the foundation of my life and the work. I am grateful to my son, Aditya for his honest and innocent appreciation. I am also thankful to my parents for their blessings and prayers.

Bhushan Khairnar

Section: 1

A Mystery of Life

Chapter: 1

"Wherever we see there is a sea, vast and deep. We sail until our hope, not ship, sink in the abysmal. Good thought, ye?"

Am read the SMS on his mobile. Some words were stronger "sea", "hope" and "abysmal". He tried to understand what Kan might mean to say. He replied,

"you r ghost, pls let me enjoy the sand"

The night was starry. The half-moon was radiating good enough light on the bare expanse of the sea coast. Am was alone on the road. He was walking towards the sea. After some distance, he saw a coconut tree and an uprooted coconut trunk. Beside the trunk, a dog was sleeping. The dog sensed the human presence around. It opened eyes, looked around, got up and stretched his body. It went towards Am. It stopped in front of him and wagged its tail. Am leant down to pat it. It misunderstood Am's posture and began to bark on him. Its eyes were furious. Out of fear, he began to walk swiftly towards the beach. Often he looked back whether the dog was following him or not. To gather the strength, he sang a popular song of his favorite album. Just after fifty meters, the dog went back to its dwelling.

Am heard the roar of the sea. He was on the beach. His mobile rang. An SMS was delivered. It was Kan again:

"A destroyed man again in the battle? A victory with a blunt sword? That's your dream? Good luck."

Kan, his intimate friend, knew the purpose of the journey. Am was in search of a meaningful way to live the life. He had read many books of self-help, religion, philosophy, biography and autobiography in hope to know the certain way to live the meaningful life. He called the way, 'the Secret'. After reading them he tried to live the life in the suggested ways and followed the ideals religiously. As a result, his life became more miserable. He was also dissatisfied with both the jobs: part-time and full-time. In last two years, he has changed five to six jobs. He had also tried to become realistic, romantic, imaginative, fanciful, rational and all possible combinations of them but he could not find the proper way. He adored the word, "optimist". After each failure, he used to watch a video, "The Secret" downloaded from YouTube. He had interpreted and reinterpreted the video hundred times.

His wife considered him eccentric. One day, she got separated from him since it was beyond her capacity to tolerate his highly optimistic behavior. The whole day, just like lovelorn, he remained gloomy and remorseful. But at night, he started the lap-top and watched the video "the secret". He believed his soul required more motivation, more positivity. He never lost his faith from the unseen secret. He always believed, there must be some secret of life. One day he would surely achieve it.

When he was surfing the free self-help eBooks, he saw an advertisement of Tourism Department of Tawai Region. In the advertisement, there were three major attractions: a tropical beach, the hotel "Taboo" and the historical place. Am read the words "The Symbols of the Secret of Life" just below the picture of the historical place. The words 'the secret of life' compelled him to search the information about the place on Wikipedia. He read the myth about the place: the symbols represent the great secret of life. If one deciphers them, he/she would be able to get whatever he/she wishes. Am searched the images of those symbols on Google. He could not find a single picture since the government of the region prohibited to carry any electronic equipment there. He immediately decided to visit the place. There was only one hotel in the nearby town. Am liked the name, 'Taboo'. He immediately booked a room in the hotel.

Next morning, he took seven days leave from both the jobs: part time and full time. He thanked God and the Universe for showing him the Omen. His intuition told him that this time he would get the secret of life.

In the evening, he initiated the long awaited journey. Tawai was almost one thousand miles away. He decided to spend the whole seven days for himself. He was desperate to know the Secret, the secret of life. He thought often to devote time to do so but circumstances didn't allow him. These seven days were devoted to this task. He was desperate this time to achieve the goal.

After reading Kan's SMS, he looked back to find whether the dog was following him or not. He was alone on the murky beach. He did not know how he would decipher the symbols of the historical place. A series of thoughts begin to flow in his mind. Since he won't be allowed to keep the mobile or any other electronic equipment with him, he decided to carry a diary with him to copy the symbols and then he would decipher them at the hotel. If needed, he would visit the place repeatedly. After all, he had seven days. What if the security won't permit him to carry the diary with him?

The sea breeze was pleasing. He put off his shoes. He experienced the wet and warm sand under his feet. He looked far deep in the sea. The tides were carrying the moon light towards him. He moved forward towards the sea water. He stopped at the spume. The aureole of the half-moon was attractive enough to grab the attention of Am. He looked at the stars. They were sharp and abundant unlike his city.

He closed his eyes, took deep breath, looked in himself, at the very moment, the sea waves touched his feet. A current ran through his body. He lost control over his senses. His body was about to explode into thousands of particles. He tried to control himself but some strange power took control over him. Every part of body and mind was moving with immense speed. He felt he was weightless and suddenly his eyes were watching the waves of the sea, rolling in and his ears were listening to his breath. Both waves and breath were in cosmic rhythm. He became conscious of the molecules and the atoms of his body which were vibrating, colliding with each other, creating new particles. They were in rhythm with the sea, the breeze and the sand. His inner eyes saw cosmic energy and rays floating around. A strange sound came from the sea and spoke, "Am". He suddenly came to conscious. He looked at himself. His head became heavy and soon lost his balance. He fell down and fainted.

Chapter: 2

Next morning, Am was awoken by the sun rays. He heard the sound of the tides. He was on the beach. He stood up, looked at the sea and cleaned the sand from his cloths. Brooding over the night experience, he went back to the hotel.

At the hotel, no one bothered to ask Am about his absence for the whole night. He went in his room and asked the servant to bring a cup of coffee. While sipping the coffee in the balcony, he tried to understand the significance of the mysterious experience of last night. He recalled Gautam Budhdha, who had similar cosmic experience and how that experience changed his life permanently. He read about it few months back.

He thought, after having such Cosmic Experience, he might have changed permanently just like Budhdha. He must have achieved the highest meaning of life. He might have the secret. But he was not sure about his achievement. So, he examined himself critically. He found that he had become more relaxed and confident. He could feel the universal energy within him. He was overjoyed.

Now, he would tell everyone, especially Kan, that he was right. There is a certain way to live the meaningful life. There is a secret. His ways were absurd but not meaningless. He would be free from every limitation. He need not require to take the help of Kan or anyone else. He would live the meaningful life hereafter. He had become perfect. He didn't require to visit the historical place. It was a great achievement. He decided to mobile Kan immediately. He wanted to share his happiness especially with him.

He entered the room with the coffee mug in right hand. When he bent down to pick up the mobile, the coffee mug slept from his hand and broke into hundreds of pieces. Very next moment, he recalled how Kan used to send him SMS when he failed to do something,

"I knew it was bound to happen. After all they are sheep. I hope you are not. Thoughts are mere fantasy until you are able to convert them into concrete reality.
Are you frustrated?
Good luck. ..."

He hesitated to pick up the mobile as he realized 'he is unable to handle this small mug; hence, he could not claim his supreme achievement'. He recalled a principle of being positive: 'One should not criticize himself/herself'. He had doubt in his mind whether his experience was the same as Buddha's cosmic experience. He opened his email inbox in his smart mobile phone. To find the received Budhha's biography, he scrolled to the older emails. Just above the biography's email, there was an email which he sent to Kan expressed his frustration when he failed to meet his expectations. He opened the email:

"God Kan,
Yesterday I felt a great motivation from inside and the day turned out pretty good.
But, today brought the same amount of depression that equaled my yesterday.

Yesterday I had a meeting with sir and he told me that when I focused on my work seriously, I achieved target. But I am not focusing CONSTANTLY on my performance. Other sir also said that I am not performing up to the mark. I instantly thought of my resignation. But I can give my resignation to the part-time job also. It's a lot headache. My throat feels dry. It's again feeling like our college days when we knew little about each other. Not alone, lonely. I am with me but partly. Most of my part resides in society, fear, anguish, world, fuck.

Death does not seem as an alternative nor fighting back, they are, but.............

I put a mirror before me and everything happened one by one, good, opposite.

FUCK.

Fuck with the boss, the head officers of all departments. Anger must relieve me.

FUCK.

I must relieve it.

FUCK.

My body feels weak, my spirit feels weak, right now I cannot stop my tears to flow from my eyes. I am crying. Yes, I am crying in the dark room of the office. sir is sitting in his office, sitting on his chair, doing some work on computer. The peon is playing Angry Bird on a pc.

Feels good, partly, relieved after crying. Skin under my eyes feel like a dry ground from which just some drops of water evaporated. I wanted to shout for last two days. FUCK.

Do not call me today, please.

Tomorrow we both will laugh together on this mail, not today.
From: nothing"
Kan replied,
"dear human,
All right, Fuck as you wish
From: Wish God"

Am was happy as he had improved a lot and he was able to tackle such situation more efficiently. He downloaded the biography and compared his experience with Budhha's. After devoting three months, Budhha had the transcendental experience. While he just had initiated his journey. "Through the last night incident, the universe has shown me an omen forecasting my success", Am thought.

He closed his eyes and thanked the universe for such wonderful cosmic experience. He got ready to visit the historical place. He took his diary with him. During the journey, he planned to utilize his time at the historical place.

At the Historical Place:

It was a huge stone monument spread in fifty acre space. There were seven huge stone chambers. After arguing for half hour, the security allowed him to keep the diary with him. The symbols were everywhere on the wall, on the roof, on the pillars and floor. He had to choose the right symbolic pattern. He had read few books on symbols and prototypical symbols suggested by Kan. He quickly examined the symbols of one chamber. He found a common pattern in the symbols of roof and floor. He rushed to other chambers and he found the same commonness. In some or other way, the symbols of all chambers were linked with each other. He drew those common symbols in his diary.

He was contended with his successful efforts. 'What you desire, you get it', Am recalled.

When he was coming out of the place, he saw the history of the place was carved on a big flat stone:
"The king, Tumayu Octave, built this place in 203 B.C. Earlier he was a merchant of dry fruit and spices. Due to his business, he travelled in both the world: East and West. In the middle-East, he met an old man who gifted him an iron plat. There were some symbols carved on it. The old man died after a day giving the plat. Due to the carved inscription, the merchant became very rich. In next few months, he became a king of a region. One day, an old man came in his drcam and askcd him to help people who desire to find the secret of life. The king obeyed the old man. The king had doubt: if he declares the secret publically, it could be misused by some people. So, he built this place and killed the 450 labors to keep the secret of the symbols. It is said that the king lived 160 years."

Am came back to the hotel, thinking over the meaning of the symbols, and cruelty of the emperor. He could not understand the proper reason behind the brutality of the emperor. He compared his boss with the emperor. "How selfish and tyrants they Are!" He recalled his fight against the system, the boss. He asked his colleagues to support his movement against the boss but the result was usual: he could not start the movement against injustice due to the lack of support. He had sent an email to Kan about the issue,

"hi Kan,
Nothing happened in the training as I planned. Only 20 per cent staff was ready to support the movement.
I liked that film. I went with my wife.
From: Am"
Kan replied in his usual style,
"Loser Winner,
I knew it was bound to happen. After all they are sheep. I hope you r not. Thoughts are mere fantasy until you are able to convert them into concrete reality.
Good luck. ..."
Enjoy the film thinking your boss. Are you frustrated?
From: Sympathy"

Am had become furious reading Kan's email. He wanted to kill, not his boss or Kan, but to himself because he believed, "Life is meaningless, he is in chain, he has no freedom since his birth. Only way to free himself was death." But he never tried to commit suicide as he was not sure whether after death he would be free or not.

He was hungry since he did not eat anything since morning. There was no food facility in the hotel. The only source of the food was the restaurant near the beach. He went towards the restaurant to have lunch. He kept diary with him. He repeatedly looked at those symbols. He was constantly trying to decipher the symbols.

After sitting at the corner table in the restaurant, he ordered the local food disc. He did not like the taste of the food. He recalled how a renowned comedian and TV artist commented on the food habit of his state people,

"People of our state are very strange, when we dine out we expect the food like home and when we dine home, we expect the food like restaurant. Each and every item, tradition, way of thinking, even language is based on the Culture of the region."

He was thinking about appropriate way to decipher the symbols. The artist's words made him think about the relation between the cultural and the symbols of the historical place. He recalled how the idea of the secret of life came to him. He often discussed about the concept of culture with Kan. Kan tried various ways to describe the concept of Culture to him,

"Culture is how we live our life in our social context. Culture is also an individual aspect because, as you know, culture plays important role in shaping an individual."

Am had many logical-illogical arguments against every explanation. He tried to get the answer from the Google but he was not satisfied with any of its answers. Finally, Kan could send him a convincing explanation:

"Do you know Lord Macaulay? He was one of the highly intellectual persons of the world who understood the power of culture. He knew how to manipulate the knowledge of culture. He was the only person who used the knowledge of culture to destroy and replace the culture. He was the first human to implement the knowledge at such bigger scale. There are certain advantages and disadvantages of being intellectual and especially, when you implement your knowledge. He is a Hero in Britain but villain in India. He destroyed Indian culture tactfully for the benefit of his country. The proof of his idea to change the Indian culture has become popular. It is attached below:

இத்தருணத்தில், சுமார் 170 ஆண்டுகளுக்கு முன்பு பிரிட்டிஷ் நாடாளுமன்றத்தின், பிரபல உறுப்பினரும், பிரிட்டிஷ் அரசாங்கத்தில் பல முக்கியப் பதவிகளை வகித்தவரும், 1834-ம் ஆண்டு பிரிட்டிஷ் அரசு அமைத்த 'சுப்ரீம் கவுன்சில் ஆஃப் இந்தியா' என்ற அமைப்பின் முக்கிய உறுப்பினருமான மெக்காலே பிரபு நான்காண்டுகள் நமது நாட்டைச் சுற்றிப்பார்த்துவிட்டு ஆங்கிலேய அரசுக்கு எழுதியதைக் கீழே தந்துள்ளோம்.

LORD MACAULAY'S ADDRESS TO THE BRITISH PARLIAMENT 2 FEBRUARY, 1835

"I have travelled across the length and breadth of India and I have not seen one person who is a beggar, who is a thief. such wealth I have seen in this country, such high moral values, people of such caliber, that I do not think we would ever conquer this country, unless we break the very backbone of this nation, which is her spiritual and cultural heritage, and, therefore, I propose that we replace her old and ancient education system, her culture, for if the Indians think that all that is foreign and English is good and greater than their own, they will lose their selfesteem, their native culture and they will become what we want them, a truly dominated nation."

Am read the explanation and he was amazed to know how one person could replace the culture and history of the world. After reading the Lord Macaulay's address, Am had begun to respect to his own culture. During that period, Am was reading a book on the secret. His imagination found a mysterious connection between the powerful, intellectual and influential person and the secret. Henceforth, he was in search of the secret of life. He read the variety of books on mysterious power, religion, symbols, motivation and so on. He believed the secret must be some sort of certain way to live the life.

Am was very excited about his new innovation. He shared his newly originated knowledge about the culture and the secret with Kan:

"your highness,

It was a nice email. I feel our culture is the best culture in the world. I respect it from bottom of my heart. But my reason is not satisfied. It asks me a question and I don't have an answer. It says that if Indian culture was that much great, then why couldn't it save itself from only one person's idea, from foreign influence?

I have one more doubt. The great and legendry people like Einstein, Newton, Hawking, And yes, Gandhiji of India, changed the world alone. How? Were they that much powerful? I don't think they were. I believe there must be some secret of life which they must not have shared with the world. I have read their biographies and auto-biographies. I felt they were hiding something from the world. I believe it was the secret of life. What's your opinion?

From: Am"

Kan replied him immediately,

"You are about to get the secret of life. Are you sure?"

Am replied,

"No, I am not sure".

Chapter: 3

"Sir, Would you like to have anything else?" the waiter said.

Am looked at his empty plate. He ordered a dark coffee. He looked at the symbols in his diary and began to think about the cultural aspects in them. He received the omen at the beach. He might get clue to decipher the symbols at the same place. Hence, he went for a short walk on the beach after finishing the coffee. It was a pleasant afternoon. He was walking along the sea water. He looked at the sea gratefully. He looked at the horizons. He was allowing the tides to touch his feet.

Unknowingly, he began to play a game with the tides. When the tide went in, he followed them, as they rolled out, he jumped high. Often he lost his balance and fell on the tide. He enjoyed it. He recalled his childhood days. How they enjoyed playing with the tides. He spent almost two hours.

Coming out of the sea, he heard the strange and mysterious sound. He turned back swiftly but no one was around. He thought it might be an illusion. Again, the same sound came from the sea. It was clearer this time. It spoke, "Am, look at your past..." When he was turning back towards the sound, a big wave knocked him down. He could not swim. He was horrified. He threw his hands and legs around. He stood up hurriedly.

Before he had recovered completely, he saw a man and a boy laughing at him. Am thought the man might be a local fisherman and the boy must be his son. He avoided them and began to walk towards the hotel. They were walking towards the coconut tree near the hotel. Am followed them. They stopped near the coconut tree and bowed down against the tree. They began to recite a prayer in their language. Am could not understand the meaning but he liked the rhyme and music of the words. Am stopped to listen to the prayer. The man looked at Am suspiciously. Then, he climbed the tree and threw two coconuts on the ground. The boy was collecting them.

Am realized, the man did not like his presence. He swanned towards the hotel. He began to think about the mysterious sound that he heard few minutes back. He could not forget the words, "Am, look at your past..."

At thc rcception, he asked not to disturb him till six in the evening. He went into his room. He was confused with the way of the universe. "What could be the significance of the sound? Is it trying to help him or mislead him? Why does it ask him to look at his past? How does it know his name? Does it mean that the symbols and his past are linked with each other?"

He never experienced such strange power of the universe. He thought, in such situation Kan would help him. Earlier he decided not to call anybody but it was totally a different situation. He put his hand in his pocket for the mobile. He realized he lost his mobile in the sea probably when he was playing with the tides or when it knocked him down. He knew it would be a useless effort to go and search his mobile. Fortunately, he kept the diary on the shore. Hence, he decided not to go and search the mobile. In fact, he was afraid of the strange power at the beach. He was not sure that it was the universal power that he read in the books or seen in the videos. He thought for a while and he impulsively spoke, "Great, the sea has taken propitiations before it grant my wish, the SECRET."

He had bought the mobile before six months. For first fourteen- fifteen days, Am cared it most. Gradually, he became used to it and he used it to read the motivational books or to watch the inspirational video. He thought "he is different from the people, the sheep. Initially they value the things then gradual devaluation and people treat their life the same way. When people begin to dream about something, it becomes the most important task in their life. But gradually, they become used to it. They begin to compromise with the process of achieving it. Finally, they alienate themselves from it. Few people remain addicted to their dream.(He liked the word 'addicted')The world recognizes them as the great people. Kan is one of them. I think I am becoming like those few people. I could devote my time to follow my dream and now, I cannot move away from my dream, the secret."

Am opened his diary. He observed the symbols closely and in back of his mind, he was thinking about the words of the mysterious sound, "Am, look at your past". He spent around fifteen minutes deciphering the symbols but he could not concentrate. He decided to give priority to the words of the mysterious sound. He thought, his past might help him to understand the symbols. He initiated the process with his childhood:

His parents were caring and loved him much in his childhood. But there was nothing significant in it. In his school days, he scored good grades but he could not make sense of what he was learning. He remained puzzled whether to ask his teacher to teach practical aspect of his learning or not. He talked about it to his friend but they considered him insane. When he was in the last year of his school days, he was very happy. He dreamed to get the answers of his all queries in his college life.

In first two weeks, he became popular as 'eccentric' in the college. He met Kan in the first year. Am was junior to Kan. Once he saw Kan giving a leaf with three leaflets to some girl. He was wishing her birthday. The girl was happy. He liked the idea and tried it on his class-mate's birthday. In the same way, he gave trifoliate to his female classmate. She threw those leaves and uttered, "Rubbish". That was one of the incidences of his failure story.

He liked Kan's unique ways. Kan appeared absurd but he was smart. He understood human psychology well. Am expected Kan would help him understanding life and himself. He decided to make him his friend. On one auspicious day, he went to meet Kan in the college canteen. He initiated the conversation with the trifoliate. He asked Kan the reason why the girl was happy receiving only leaf? Kan replied he had given the flower day before.

At the end of the semester, Kan asked Am to perform the role of an absurd character. He loved the idea. He never performed before. But he liked the story much.

Am recalled how Kan wrote a play based on Samuel Beckett's "Waiting for Godot" and how they performed it. Kan told him he wrote it to satirize their institute's culture and its meaningless traditions. The play was appreciated by all except faculty members. The play:
"Kan was performing the role of Bruno, wearing old and torn cloths. Am was performing the role of Digo, wearing torn jacket and dirty blue jeans.

The play began with the speech of Bruno. He showed his hand which was shivering. Bruno told the audience,
"Look my hand is shivering with fear, Look! I am afraid of you. Look at this roof. It has become old. Are you?"

On stage, there was only one tree having three leaves on it. On right there was one oil-ken and exactly beside it there was a small half broken chair.

Am entered and asked Kan to initiate the play. Kan stared at Am and spoke loudly to drop the curtain. They went to the back-stage. When the curtain was raised, Am was lying flat on the stage. He was fully covered with a dirty cloth. Kan moved towards him, watched him carefully. He was worried. He thought Am must have died. He went close to Am and asked him a question,
"Are you dead?"
Am got up without opening his eyes and said, "Yes" and he lay again.
Kan (anxiety on face), "Are you sure?"
Am got up thinking and in confused voice, he said,
"No, I am not sure."

He stood up and began to walk in circle. He increased the speed gradually. Kan moved towards the oil-ken and sat on it. He starred the audience. Am felt giddy and shambled to sit beside Kan. He tried to fit himself on the small chair but it was too small for him. He often lost his balance and fell down. He complained to Kan. Kan tried to motivate him. Am looked at the chair suspiciously and moved towards the center of the stage. He jumped high. He spoke loudly to Kan, "I am dying." And he lay down.

Kan looked at Am and spoke with anxiety, "Are you sure?"

Am, "Yes, I am sure."

Kan walked to him, covered him with the dirty cloth and asked, "Are you dead?"

Again the same scene, Am got up and said, "Yes"

Kan, "Are you sure?"

Am, "No, I am not sure. I am dead. I think I am. But I am not sure."

The play was about such similar scenes: search of the tradition and culture and they called a stone "tradition", and the play ended with their efforts to stop breathing as they extended their hands towards the institute building."

The play became popular among the students. Everyone began to call them Bruno and Digo. Then after, whenever they could not reach any solution, they used to end the conversation with the dialogues of the play, "Are you sure?" and "not sure".

Am believed his life is like the play. He was never sure about anything.

After completion of the university education, he applied for many jobs. Most of the time, he did not get reply from the companies. Even if someone would call him for an interview, he was rejected within few minutes. He sent an email to Kan about his struggle to get a job. Kan asked him to send him his resume. Kan sent his own resume as a sample. Am realized he did not know how to write a resume.

Am realized his past was not helpful in deciphering the symbols. It was a waste of time. He recalled the words of the mysterious sound at the beach, "Am, look at your past." He told himself, "All right, I need to peep further in my life for the more meaningful experience." He contemplated for a while and came to conclusion that his conversation with Kan, especially about his life, might be more meaningful. Both Am and Kan expressed their views on life through the series of emails:

"Real Am ,

My Last Four Days:

Past has its' own whims, may be my past does not. I went to the college with my eyes and leaving my shoulder at home. I kept the body parts somewhere in the heaven. When I came back in the evening I was accompanied by head which was in pain. Emotions were crushing my neurons. I believe I recognized myself that evening. Moral of last four days:After Dirty Picture there is always M. F. Hussain Because he left India since long back.

From: Emotional Head"

Am liked the way of Kan. He was always philosophical. Am understood the initial portion but he could not understand the moral. Am knew M. F. Hussain is a famous painter of India, and the circumstances in which M. F. Hussain had to leave his country painfully. Am could not only understand the conjunction, "because". But he took it as a challenge and he began to work over it. Finally, he found two possible answers. He sent them to Kan,

"Stressed philosopher,

Initially I thought you have committed an error in using the conjunction "because" but you are tricky. I understood what you meant. I thought there are two possible meaning of the moral. They are given below:

a. "Dirty Picture" represents the controversial paintings of Mr.Hussain and because of which he left India.

b. Mr. Hussain is an artist. He was in such traumatic situation where he could not compromise with his artistic ideals. So, he knew from the beginning that someday he would have to leave India, his mother land. You are in similar situation.

Second one is more appropriate. Am I right?

How are you now? What happened?

Inform me...

From: Winner"

Kan's reply was usual,

"Caring Winner,

I confess it was an error. I used wrong conjunction. But it's nice. How an error could be more meaningful than the correct use of the words or the proper way of conveying the ideas.

I am fine now. I have chosen un-trodden way.

From: Made philosopher"

Am was not ready to accept Kan's reply. He felt it was his chance to win. He worked and thought hard to find the answer. In fact, Am for the first time could reply with such deep, logical and meaningful understanding. He began to find an appropriate reply to this tricky and dishonest reply of Kan. He read Kan's email several times about M. F. Hussain. He could figure out some absurd and strong ideas. Now, he had to find appropriate words for his ideas. Am believed that he could think and understand great ideas but it was very difficult for him to implement or to find words for it. After many efforts, he found satisfactory words. He emailed Kan,

"Dear Tricky Fellow,

I know world is round. Don't try to make me fool. Accept that you are defeated. You are very meticulous at choosing words. You can't commit such stupid error.

I am giving you one puzzle to solve:

My clothes r wearing me, my bike is driving me, a cup of coffee is drinking me and now a cursor is writing me. What will u say about me? I am waiting for your reply.

From; think tank"

Kan was busy working on some serious issue of his research, when he received the email of Am on his smart-phone. Kan read the email and replied without giving much thought.

"Dear existentialistic Judge,

I look at coffee not at cup while it is life. I look at cup while it is coffee.

I accept my defeat. You are good one. Are you sure?

From: "Coffee drinker but tea lover"

Finally, Am accepted his defeat as Kan was beyond his understanding.

Am tried to fall in love but either the girl would not show her interest in him or some good fellow would take her away. Still he believed he never lost interest from the girls and as a proof he got married. He struggled to keep his wife happy. He never understood what she wanted. Finally, he accepted, "No man can understand woman". His wife considered him whimsical and unpractical. She left him just two weeks before.

He could not accept the conventional ways of his parents, their beliefs, and their traditions. He wanted to live more meaningful life. It was his fifth job in his two years career. He could not find meaning in his routine.

Am wanted to know the meaning of the symbols as early as possible. He lost his passions. He decided to analyze the symbols of the historical place without wasting time in meaningless past. He opened the diary and looked at the symbols. After intensive analyses, he found three common symbols: round, square and triangle and all symbolic cycles were in the seven stages. He tried to figure out the meaning but it was difficult task to bring out meaning from these basic symbols as they had thousands of possible meanings.

Chapter: 4

An idea sparkled in his mind. It was subconscious which might help him. He learnt to take help of subconscious. He sat for the brain-storming which would help him to understand the symbols and the secret. He sat with ball-pen and his diary. He closed his eyes and took deep breath for thirty seconds. He asked himself to calm down. He began to focus within. He forgot what to do then. He began to scold himself for not practicing the method after learning it from Kan. He recalled the words of Kan,

"You should be able to take decisions by yourself. So, learn this trick and you would be able to use your subconscious."

Am experienced the presence of some strange power around. He focused on recalling the method of taking help of subconscious. He closed his eyes. He thought to sleep instantly. He recalled the first stage: "Close your eyes and imagine you are sleeping and simultaneously observe yourself from outside."

Am observed he was moving deep into some mysterious dark tunnel. He wandered in his body with amazement. When he reached at the fingers, he felt some heavy object was carried by him. He tried hard to identify the object. He recalled it must be the pen. In fraction of second he reached mind where thousands of thoughts were flowing in and out. He tried to recognize those thoughts. His hands began to move. He could not understand exactly what he was doing.

After some time, he opened his eyes, looked at the diary, the pages were full with the scattered words:

"Children,-movies-day, dreaming-social functions, death, birth, pollution-listerning music- driving- see pictures, sculpteres, trying to create imperation, getting impressed-learning new things-forgetting things-reading news papers-watching TV-daydream-feeling jealous-drawing-doctors and hospitals-taking care of mine and others-using mobile, net, computer,-read news-paper-sitting under tree- remembering family members, thinking about them positively and negatively-shaving-banks-fearing with different things and people-reading faviourites, thinking about them-taking decisions-writing things-feeling senses of mine and others-thinking about death, watching someone die, getting birth-river-speaking- from atm,-buying goods-sleeping- Communication with people-quarrels -eating,-love profit sometimes lose-failure success-drinking coffee with roti-lunch-dinner-wander-think-drinking water-giving and receiving information-getting angry-washing hands-little tricks to spread happiness,humourous comments and uses of regular common life's incidents with the use of material things around us, taking breadth, eyes opening close etc.-things related to senses-laziness-desires-loneliness-eyes-escape from a situation-finding ways to get benefits-money saving stretagies,to follow them ,desert them-seeing lizards eating mosquitoes-befool someone-going libraries-talking to friends-thinking on material and other things-doing ironing-trying to find new ways of helping myself-thinking on physic and its differences and similarities with others-animals and other existing beings-mystery-

darkness-night-hidden and open worlds-light-garment its patterns,colours effect of all these material things on me and us-fire and thoughts-females and males-forms of admission-thinking as an absurd-patriotism-songs my country, braviourу, valour, courage, love, rising, growth

and at the same time enter in it objectively-age-measured use of language-obstacles- invisible in visible-money-sacred places-importance of memory-ethics-follow with nd without thinking-generation differences-skin of snake-eyes-idiot ness-social, formal behavior-why challenge-immorality-I-search for an explanation about my existence."

He looked at the diary. He looked at the jumbled words. They were indicating many stages and various occasions of life. They were meaningful as well as absurd. There were some spelling errors, incomplete and meaningful sentences. It was reflecting his own life and from the other perspective, it was about all people whom he knew. He realized how his subconscious was able to express divert thoughts, how it was able to convert thoughts into the words. Totality is meaningless but if we look at each word, it is meaningful. From surface level to abysmal, our mind is linked with thoughts.

Am knew it since long but today he experienced it. The symbols: round, square and triangle began to make sense.

Someone knocked the door. Am got distracted. He lost the meaningful thought sequence. He got up, opened the door and shouted at the hotel servant,

"I told you not to disturb me until six..."

The servant was surprised. He replied politely,
"Sorry sir, but it is six thirty now."
Am looked at his watch. It was six-thirty. He could not believe he spent three hours in brain-storming. He asked the servant to bring coffee for him.

He went back to the diary. The same sequence of the words which were significant suddenly became meaningless. He focused to link with his unconscious but he realized it was useless then.

Am put the diary in the bag believing it might help him in future to understand the secret. He saw the lap-top in the bag. He took it out and decided to play some music or the motivational film, 'The Secret'. He opened the song list but he could not decide which songs he should play. He opened a game, Angry Bird and began to play it. He recalled how the peon in the officc was expert at playing it and the only tough competitor was his Boss. Both were the idlest fellows in the organization. There was a knock on the door. It was the servant with a cup of tea. He apologized to Am for not having coffee and they would manage to get it by next morning. Am did not say anything and went into the balcony to have the tea. The tea was dark and sugarless. He liked its bitterness. He did not like tea earlier. Kan used to force him to drink tea. One day Am asked Kan why he adored tea. Kan looked at him, observed Am's intention and gave reply,

"Tea, it is opium. What you drink is not important. What the taste or the quality is also not important. When you are among your friends, TEA gives us chance to share our ideas, opinions; especially it allows us to empty our heart. And when we are alone, it gives us space to think over life, about ourselves. The richness lies in the concept not in the object, tea."

After finishing the tea, Am sat near the lap-top. He took the diary out and observed the symbols again. He tried to decipher them. After five minutes, he shut down the lap-top and he got ready to move out.

Am kept the diary with him. He went to the beach. His determination to know the certain meaningful way to live the life instigated him to be at the beach. The mysterious experience of yesterday night came on surface. He shivered. He began to think about the symbols and his past.

The sea was calm that night. He saw the stars in the sky, the moon and the waves travelling on the waves. He sat near the water. He listened to the sound of the waves. He loved the bright stars. At his home town, he used to spend at least one hour with the stars on the terrace of his home.

To relieve the unbearable stress Am shouted,

"Hey, I am here, come on, reply me. I am here to get the secret. What secret do you want to convey?"

There was no response. He went in the water, looked in all direction. Only the tides were rolling out and in. He calmed himself down. He recalled the words of Steve Jobs, great innovator and pioneer in i-pad series,

"Live the day as if it was the last day of your life."

He was determined to get the clue to decipher symbols that night. He would stay there until the mysterious universal power helped him.

He came out of the water. He waited for next two hours but no response. He observed the sand, the water, spume, and everything which attracted his senses. To kill time, he prepared a sand-hill. He tried to carve a cave in it. He failed often and thought that when he was child, he liked to prepare sand-hill and used to prepare a cave in it. But he was never able to construct the cave successfully. When he would fail he thought, "When he will grow up, he will be able to make it easily."

Now he was grown up still he could not prepare a cave in sand-hill. Am became busy in preparing the cave. He took it as a challenge. He used the dry and wet sand. He prepared a sand fence to protect the sand-hill from the sea waves. Finally, he succeeded to carve a cave in the sand-hill. He was contended and pleased with the success. Kan used to tell him that if we focus on small achievements, one day we become able to achieve the great. Am thought Kan was right.

He realized he was becoming impatient to know the secret. He had forgotten everything else. The quest became his life. He looked towards the water. A bright point of light was emerging at the horizon of the sea. It was becoming larger. Am stood up. Before he could understand anything, the figure was at in front of him:

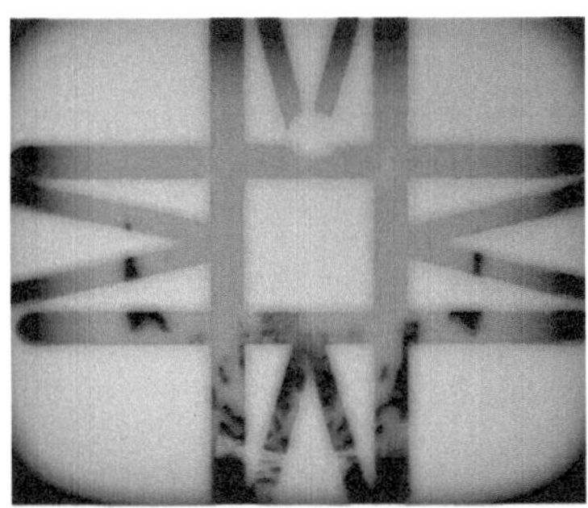

Because of its brightness, Am could not see the figure clearly. Very next moment, he was surrounded by the figure. He was in the center of the square. It was squeezing. He was horrified. He used all his strength to come out of it. The figure broke into many small particles. The shapes of the particles were round, square and triangle. They disappeared in the dark sky. Before it disappeared, he heard the mysterious sound. Am could not understand what it uttered. His body became much heavier and he fell unconscious.

Chapter: 5

A dog was barking. Am opened his eyes. He was on the beach. It was still murky. He heard the sound of the tides. It was dawn. Something touched his left foot. It was rectangle in shape. He sat down and stretched his arm to pick up the thing. It was a mobile. He observed it closely. He was surprised it was his own mobile which he lost there. He cleaned it. It was not in working condition. Still he put it in his pocket.

The barking of the dog became louder. He looked towards the sound. The dog was running towards him. He thought it might attack him. He stood up swiftly. The dog was looking back as if something was chasing it.

Am tried to see what was behind it. It was not followed by anything still the dog was continuously barking towards the direction. He waited for few minutes. But nothing appeared. He assumed there might be a wild animal. The dog stopped keeping safe distance from Am. The dog expected Am's company but it was not sure whether Am would allow him or not. He slowly went towards the dog, petted on head. The dog wagged its tail.

Am sat down near it and the dog sat around one foot away. Am began to think about the mysterious power, yesterday's experience. The dog slept keeping faith in Am. There was a creeping sound coming from the direction of the coconut tree. The dog rose and ran towards the sound swiftly.

Instead of going back to the hotel, Am went in the water. He saw a group of fishes jumping out of the water and the sun rays were reflected through their skin. For the first time in his life, he felt from within how the life is beautiful. But he could not forget the mysterious experience of last night. He recalled the symbols of the historical place. The prototypes were round, square and triangle. The same symbols, he saw yesterday night. There might be some link between the symbols and the figure. Am was sure that the universe was helping him, giving him clue to decipher the symbols.

After some time, he walked back to the hotel. When he reached the coconut tree, he saw the dog was sleeping. He thought, "The poor soul did not sleep last night". Then he realized it was not breathing. He went closer to it. He examined it carefully. It was dead.

Am could not understand the reason. The dog came to him to urge him to save his life. Am could not understand the dog. Am began to find the clues. He saw blood stain on the head of the dog. He presumed that it might have been hit by some vehicle. He saw two coconuts half buried into the sand. There was blood stain on one of the coconuts. Now, he conjectured the coconut might have fallen on it and it died.

Section: 2

The Coconut Man and the Tree

Chapter: 6

He reached the hotel. There was crowd outside the hotel. Among them, there were the government officers and the policemen who were shouting at the hotel manager. He could not understand the complete conversation but he conceived that they were talking about crime at the hotel.

Overlooking them, Am moved towards his room. He was stopped by the police. They questioned him. Am tried to explain them that he had proofs of his identity but they were in his bag. Two police officers followed him. He opened the room. They entered it but the room was empty. There was no bag, no lap-top, nothing. Am could not figure out what was going on. He did not have word to speak. He complained the police-officers about the issue. They looked at him. Discussed with each other and instructed him,

"We are not arresting you because we believe that you are innocent. We won't take you to the police-station but you cannot leave the town without prior permission of the officials. Your luggage is in our custody. You will be given back only after the investigation gets over."

Am argued that he did not have enough money with him. He should be allowed to take his credit and debit cards. But no one bothered to listen to him. He became frustrated. He lost his mobile; he lost his identity proofs and his luggage. Am did not know what he would do. He decided to call his father. He began to search a telephone booth. He asked a local fellow, part of the crowd, about the telephone booth. He told him that it was near beach. Am laughed at his fate and spoke aloud,

"It must be that strange power, it must be controlling me, it wants me to be there at the sea."

He decided to face the strange power. He went towards the beach. He reached at the provision shop near the beach. A telephone was kept on the wooden counter. The shop-keeper was reading a local newspaper. Am asked the shop-keeper whether the phone was working or not. He nodded without looking at Am. Am picked up the receiver, dialed home. Am's heart was throbbing fast. Somebody picked it up. His father spoke, "Yes, who is there?"

Am was happy. He described everything to his father. He asked him to do something immediately. Suddenly, the voice of the father began to change. Am could not listen to him properly. There was silence. He raised his voice. There was no response. He was about to put the receiver down, he heard some familiar sound. It was not his father's voice. It was the same sound that he heard at the sea. It spoke,

"Am, I have the secret"

Am shouted,

"Who are you? Do you really want to help me? Why do you hide yourself? Come and talk to me. Tell me where do you want me to meet you? I am not scared of you. You have taken away everything from me. Still I believe you are the universal power. Are you?"

There was no response. He put the receiver down in frustration. In fact, he was horrified. He asked the shop-keeper the call charges.

The shop-keeper replied keeping his head buried in the news-paper,
"Sorry sir, we don't charge for the dead phone"
And he laughed at Am. Am could not believe his words and picked up the receiver swiftly. It was dead. He shook it, tapped it hard but it was not working. Am thought people here are strange and the things are more. That day coconut man and his son were laughing and today this shop-keeper. The place itself is mysterious. The shop-keeper explained,
"Sir, I forgot to tell you. There was some problem with the telephone connections. It will be restored after four days."
Am asked himself to calm down and remain positive. "The power is in present moment", he recalled the sentence of one of the self-help books. He decided to fight back and face the mysterious power on the beach.

Chapter: 7

He saw the coconut man and the boy near the coconut tree. He instinctively went there shouting, "Santiago, I am coming".

Am subconsciously compared Santiago, the main character of "The Alchemist" with the coconut man.

The coconut man and the boy did not pray that day. The man asked the boy something in their local tongue. The boy took few leaps and picked up one dry coconut which was lying five to six feet away from the dog. The boy saw the blood spot on the coconut. The boy shouted and threw the coconut on the ground. The man went towards the boy and began to speak in slower tone.

Am did not know their language. He could not understand anything. But he became curious to know what they were talking. Am went near to them. The man looked at Am. He understood Am's eagerness. The man initiated the conversation in English,

"The dog died becos that coconut fell on head last night. We not came yesterday because the boy illness. And his illness passed to the dog. So, it died. Our god coconut tree saved his life. But poor animal... It love us, love us lot."

Am did not know how to respond. He looked puzzled. The man said,

"You think. I know Englis how? Many visitor come and go. Some are very good. They give money and teach us their englis. I ask the boy learn englis but he not listen me."

Am looked at the boy. He turned his face away. Am told the man,

"Your son is nice. He helps you a lot. Do you come here to collect coconuts every day?"

The coconut man,

"Yes, every day. We collect them and keep them in our house. We have fifty coconut tree there in our place. My farm is nice but this tree is our god. See, it has saved my sons life. He was ill last night. I prayed our God to save his life. Our God is sea and this tree (pointing towards the coconut tree). I saw dream yesterday night. This tree was talking in my dream. It told me that if you want to save your son's life, you give me gift in return. I am poor man. I don't have anyone in this world. I prayed it to save his life."

Am listened to him with interest. The boy picked up another coconut which was half buried just behind the coconut tree. He was happy to bring it to the man. He showed it to him. The man appreciated the boy. He did not climb the tree that day. The man and the boy discussed some matter with each other. Am could not understand it.

They dug a dig near the tree. They dragged the dog and threw it in the dig. They also buried both the coconuts with the dog. They put dry coconut leaves on the grave of the dog. The man looked at Am. He asked Am to put some dust on the grave. He obeyed the man. Am assumed that the man might know the reason of the dog's death. He expressed his doubt,

"Yesterday I spent my night on the beach. The dog came there. It was afraid of something. It was barking towards this direction. Is there any wild animal around?"

Am noticed a sudden change of the man's expression. He looked offended. The man did not answer Am. He started to walk towards the beach. He asked his son to follow him. Am hurriedly followed them. Am asked apology to the man for the inadequate question. He tried to convince the man that he did not meant to offend them or their rituals. The man stopped. He looked at Am and asked him to follow them if he wanted to know the answer. Am thought for a while and he began to walk behind them. The boy suddenly looked worried about something. Am wanted to ask him the reason but he thought it is better to keep his mouth shut.

For first fifteen minutes, they did not talk with each other. They were walking along the sea water. Finally, Am asked the man a question to break the silence,

"How far is your home from here?"

The man,

"Just ten minutes. (Examining Am) Are you tired? Do you drink water?"

Am understood he meant if he wanted water.

Am replied politely,

"Yes, but I am not tired. We shall continue with our journey."

The man giving him water,

"Visitors do not understand the sea but it understands everyone."

Am realized his grave tone. He replied,

"You people live with the sea. You sense it every moment. It must be talking to you."

Am thought he should not have talked about it. The man might consider him insane. He composed himself and hurriedly,

"I mean you understand it in better way because you experience it every day."

The man without changing his expression,

"True, we pray it as well. But sometime we find it strange, very strange. It behave mystery. We are afraid of it sometime. But it is our life. We live in our own way."

Am smiled and thought, "Not only the sea but the whole place was mysterious. I might get my answer through this man. It might be the purpose of the universe to send me with this pure hearted man. The place has given me a chance to find the most awaited and the most precious gift, the secret..."

The man interrupted Am's thought,

"Sir, what you do at your place? Where are you come?"

Am,

"My name is Am. Call me Am, not sir. I am from Tifal city. It is one thousand miles from here."

The man,

"You have your house?"

Am could not understood the significance of such strange question. He observed himself. His cloths were dirty and he did not comb his hair. He realized he looked like beggar. He had never been like that. But he was contended with the internal beauty, with his quest. He realized he had not yet answered the man. He looked at the man and gave reply,

"I look like beggar because since last night I lost everything here and might gain the most precious thing of my life. Yes, I have a big house at Tifal. I have been caught in strange situation here. Here officials are not allowing me to go back to my place. I stayed in the hotel near beach. Something wrong happened in the hotel. It was raided by the police and I was thrown out of it and all the more, I was not given my luggage, not even my credit and debit cards. I was left with little money in this strange place. Here phones are not working. But I liked the beautiful nature here. The sea is great but strange."

The man could not understand everything but he could sense what he meant. After few minutes, he spoke,

"Sir, we don't understand cred card and some other card that you speak. But you are alive and free. You must thank your god. Life is beautiful. Yes, tears are part of life but happiness worth more."

Am was surprised to hear such highly philosophical words from the Coconut man whose life was limited to the coconuts and the sea. Am nodded and said,

"You are right. I should thank my god. I should thank Kan."

The man,

"Ken is your God?"

Am,

"Yes and no. Kan is my friend. He has always helped me. He has always helped me to understand life. I could not understand him completely and he knew it as well. He never complained about my insane deeds."

The man,

"He is very close to you. You have wife? How many childrens?"

Am,
"I am married. My wife works in the corporate office like me but she left my home two weeks before. I have no child yet. What about you?"
The Man pointing towards a hut,
"Look! That is our house. I lost everything except this boy."

Chapter: 8

Am wanted to know the reason but before he asked about it, the man began to narrate his life story,

"I had two son and two girl. On one night, we both this son and I were sleeping outside our house. The wind was fast. All coconut trees were moving here and there so fast. My wife told me to sleep in the house but I told her I am safe. I asked this boy to go and sleep with his mother but he said no. He like to sleep in open air. He like the stars and the moon. One big coconut tree near our house fall on our house and at that moment a very big wave of the sea, came towards us. I did not know what to do. I climbed that coconut tree carrying this son. It was very big. It took away everything."

Am turned towards the sea. It was almost fifty meters away from the hut. He tried to understand the sea, the mysterious power, its cruelty. Am thought he had to teach the man how to live the life positively. He wanted to tell the man, "You are responsible for your present life. Your thoughts have attracted the good or bad thing in your life. So, do not blame the sea, the coconut tree or anything else." But he did not.

The man asked him to sit down. Am sat down on a wooden platform outside the hut. The man offered a coconut to Am. He accepted it with gratitude. The boy was happy to be at home. He looked at Am as if he was sympathetically unhappy about him. Am could not understand the reason. Am gave him ten bucks. The boy accepted it joyfully and ran away towards the sea.

The man told the boy something in their tongue. The man, looking at Am,
"He gone to play with his friends. He will come back on evening."
Am ,
"Will he not come back to have his lunch?"
The man,
"He eat it with his friends. Do not worry. He likes that."
Am looked at the man,
"Do you still have faith in the sea, the tree?"
The man,
"You see, my wife and my childrens died because of the coconut tree but the same coconut tree saved our life. It gives us food. We sell coconuts and earn money. On next day when the storm calm down, we tried to search our family but it was lost. It went into the sea. We built temporary house and next day, we gone to the coconut tree which is near your hotel. There were two trees but on the same night one of the tree fell down. There is mysterious relation between that tree and our trees here. I know you will not believe me. But it's true."

The man did not wait for Am's response. He went in his house for some work. Am began to think about the secret that he was seeking. He thought he has attracted this man, this situation. Now, he should be positive and focused towards his goal, the secret. He looked around. There was a coconut farm around twenty five meters away. He went to see the farm. As he entered the farm, the leaves of the coconut began to rustle. He immediately moved out of the farm. The leaves stopped rustling. Next moment, the earth began to shake. It was an earthquake.

The man rushed out of the hut and asked Am,
"Sir, are you ok? Do not be afraid. Nature is like that only. When sinners increase on the earth, the nature shakes them out of it."

Am nodded and sat down near the coconut tree. The man went back into the hut. He recalled the morning incident. He recollected the yesterday night incident of the dog. The dog might have got afraid of the tree when a coconut might have fallen down on the earth and it came to him. But when it went back another coconut might have fallen on it and that must be the reason behind the death of the dog.

He saw the man coming out of the hut, brought some tribal food. He served it to Am. He loved the taste.

The man,
"Now, I have to do lots of work today. There are many coconuts he need to cut from the tree. Two coconuts from the each tree. I need to climb all fifty. The dog died because he went there second time. The poor fellow."

Am,
"Why do you need to climb every tree? There are lots of coconuts on all of them. You will be able to save your time and energy. Is there any other specific reason to climb on every tree and cut only two? Am I wrong?"

The man,
"I told you in the morning. That coconut tree is our god. It care our life. Only we need to understand

omens. Only two coconut fell from the tree. So, I need to cut only two"
Am could not understand what he wanted to convey. The man continued,
"It was a pleasant day. We, this boy and I, went to pray to that coconut tree in the morning. There were two coconut trees before. But when we reach there, one tree was fall down. Only one tree was alive. Before we understand anything, the rain begin to fall. We came back without coconut that day. It was told us about the night incidence. I loss my childrens and wife. But we could not understand. From that day, it is our ritual to cut the same numbers of coconuts which we cut at the god tree. Today, the fate has this plan for me."

Am listened him patiently. He was trying to make sense of every incident. He was confused since morning. He did not the answer why he was asked to follow the man. Why they did not like his question about the dog this morning. Finally, he asked him the reason for his rude behavior in the morning.

The man did not reply and went back into the hut. Am did not know how and what response to be given in such situation. He kept mum. The man went to the farm and climbed a tree. Am went behind him. The man asked him not to worry about him. It was his routine work. Am told him,
"I want to kill my time. I may not be good like you but I will try my best. Tell me where to put these coconuts."
There were five buckets. The man pointed towards them. Am,

"Right, your maths is good. Twenty in each basket. But how will you sell them?, Who will buy them? How will you transport them alone? You alone cannot do it. Is there any town nearby?"

The man,

"No, no town nearby. But don't worry. The nature cares us, if we have faith in it. It plans in advance for us. It knows everything. So, not to worry. It is always there to take care. I do not know how but I know if that coconut tree has given us hundred coconuts, it will give us some solution. The sea is like that only."

Am wanted to talk about the positive attitude but he recalled the words of Kan,

"Let them be themselves and you are free."

He heard sound of a vehicle. It was a small goods carriage. A big man got down from it and walked straight to the coconut man. The man asked him to wait for few minutes. He would fill the buckets in no time. Am could see the worry on the man's face. Am,

"Don't worry. We are two today. Your tree has arranged it for you. You cut the coconuts and I will collect them. Do you know this fellow?"

The coconut man,

"Yes, from last two years. He comes here every fifteen days to buy our coconuts. He will be happy today to get hundred coconuts. He many times complaints about less coconut but this time he will be happy."

Am,

"How much he pays for coconuts?"

The man,

"He pays good money. For every ten he pays two bucks. We don't need to worry about transportation and sell them on the beach. It is a great relief to us. And we are only two. My boy is small. He is god's man."

Am wanted to tell him immediately,

"The big man is exploiting you. He is paying very less."

But he asked himself not to interfere in other's life. He controlled his desire and gave smile to the man. Am focused on collecting the coconuts.

After fifteen minutes, the big man went away with the coconuts in the carriage. Both were tired. The sun was already in the west. Am thought he should move back to the beach. He should spend some time with himself. He needed to think over many issues of his own life. He must find the secret.

He asked the man about the boy. The man replied that the boy would remain with his friends until the sun set. He asked the man if he had an extra coconut or not. He wanted to drink the coconut water. The man nodded and went in the hut. Am looked the man going into the hut. He desired to see the hut from inside. He shouted,

"Listen! May I come in with you?"

The man gravely,

"Sir, I would have allowed you but today the dog died and the ghost of the death is still inside the hut. I cannot allow you to take risk. It is better you keep yourself away from it. You have saved my life, probably my son's life."

The man came out with five coconuts. He offered one to Am. Am drank it gratefully. He was contended. Am,

"Thank you for nice coconut and the day that you have spent with me. I am going to the same beach where we met today morning. If life permits me, I will visit your house again."

The man whispered,

"True, if life permits..."

The man went near the farm. He looked at the sky. He stopped at a coconut tree. He touched it as if he wanted to tell it, 'you are wonderful.' Am was happy to see it. He liked the way of fare well. The man remained dispassionately detached.

Chapter: 9

He was walking along the sea. The sound of its tides was clear. He liked the warm breeze. He had spent meaningful time with the man. Earlier he did not know who the coconut man was. But now, he knew him better. He spent the whole day with him. Am was carrying four coconuts, a diary and a mobile.

His right hand began to ache. He was exhausted. He carried four coconuts with it. On other hand, he had his diary in which he had recorded the history of the quest for the secret. He lost the grip over the diary and it fell open. When he leant down to pick up the diary, he saw a conch. He liked it. He picked it up. It was small. He knew how to whistle it. He pressed it between middle and ring finger. He kept it on the lower lip, rounded the tongue and took a deep breath and blew the air from the teeth passage. The air went in the conch and took circular flow and flew out with a peculiar sharp sound as if it was imitating the sea breeze. Am told the diary,

"The conch has the same waves but one need to blow energy into it. It will become the breeze."

Am saw an open page in the diary. A word 'dog' caught his eyes. He tried to understand the real reason. His mind was not ready to accept the coconut man's logic for the dog's death. He thought it was mere a coincident. But two coconuts from every tree! Was it logical? The coconut man might understand it well. He was like this conch which had become part of his world. He lived here from his birth probably. He did not ask about it. Oh! He had forgotten to ask even his name.

Am thought the coconut man was living in the rhythm with the sea. He was sharing the same waves and energy. But he was not a happy man. He lost his family. It could mean that to be poor and live close to the Nature does not give you assurance of happiness. He was honest but ignorant but does the knowledge give guaranty of happiness? The big man was exploiting him but he did not even realize it. It might be teaching me that ignorance is bliss sometime.

He opened the diary and read few pages of it. He was repeatedly considering himself lucky. He got chance to experience Nature so close. Then he told himself,

“Am, the visit to the coconut man might help him in understanding the secret. The life has infinite number of experiences yet to be unfolded.”

He reached the beach at the time of the sun set. The sun was moving behind the sea periphery. The air blew faster and the sand particles began to fly with it. Am could not close his eyes in time. He put the coconuts down and the diary beside them. He immediately rubbed his eyes still the irritation in both the eyes was unbearable. He could not use the sea water. It would cause more irritation in them. He realized he had the coconuts given by the coconut man.

He decided to wash his eyes with coconut water. He did not know whether he would fill better or it would become worst. He used a stone lying around to open the skull of the coconut. He sprinkled the water in his eyes. He felt better. He thanked the coconut man.

He looked towards the sea. He heard the strange and mysterious sound coming nearer to him. He recognized it. It was the same sound that he heard on the first day and he felt it is the same power which was responsible for all the mysterious experiences. The sound became clearer and louder. It spoke,

"Am, have you looked at your past? Have you understood the significance of it?"

Am looked in all directions. He tried to identify from where the sound was coming. But he could not. He heard whispering sound. He was so puzzled that he did not listen to the words of the mysterious power properly. He tried to recollect what was said by the mysterious power.

Earlier he decided to ask the mysterious power many questions about the happenings and wanted to show his intensive desire for the secret. But when it was in front of him, he lost all his senses. He stood freeze. The mysterious sound repeated the questions in the same manner,

"Have you understood the significance of your past?"

Am thought for a while and gave reply confused,

"There is nothing significant in my past. But...but why do you ask me these questions? How do you know my name?"

The mysterious sound interrupted and asked him to calm down. Am obeyed the command and asked himself to calm down. The mysterious sound replied,

"Am, I like your name. Your name suggests existence. One should know why he/she exists. You tried to find the answer. You wanted to know the mystery of life as you call it “the secret of life”. I want to help you to find your answer. And yes, don’t worry. I won’t harm you. I never harm anyone”

Am,

“But how do you know me, my quest?”

The mysterious sound,

“I exist for those people who ask this question, about the secret of life. I am creation of their thoughts, desires, feelings and the universe. I am created by both human and the universe. I am here because you desired the answer and the universe wanted to answer your question. I am your creation. The universe has created me for you.”

Am could not put faith in the mysterious sound yet. But his heart wanted to trust it. He looked towards the sea and spoke,

“I can’t understand what you say. Kindly elaborate it. Give some examples. I understand better through examples.”

The mysterious sound,

“Can you listen to the sound of the waves? But before few second did you listen to it? The sound was always there but before few seconds you didn’t desire to listen it and now you are listening to it because you desire to. Similarly if you desire something, you will get it.”

Am,

“But people desire many things but their desires are not fulfilled.”

The mysterious power,

“People think about it and at the same time, they also think the reasons why they do not deserve it. You experienced the rhythm of universe and your own rhythm. You must have observed that many particles were created and many were destroyed at the same moment. Desire results into creation but when it is prevented it is destroyed."

Am,

"But, I could not understand what you have said just now."

The mysterious power,

"When your body is in rhythm, both the processes help body to maintain its form. When a child grows, his creation processes is faster than negation. So we realize his growth, while opposite is applied to the old people. Now, I will explain you the concept of negative and positive.

When your body receives the desire of negation, it increases the contradiction process. Our body puts additional effort to keep the balance. But if the negation increases beyond certain point, body decides to allow specific area to get damaged which people feel in the form of pain or disease. Because of this misbalance, people felt negation as negative term. They began to dislike negative. Out of this dislike they focus more on negative. The result is obvious. They become unhealthier from the mind and the body."

Am became eager to know further. He could understand what was told by the mysterious power. He thought it is the only chance to get the answer of his ultimate quest. But he wanted to confirm the authenticity of the mysterious power. So, he asked,

"Tell me how do you come into existence? Explain in brief, please."

The mysterious sound,
"I need to take help of quantum physics to explain you how I come into existence. You might have read the experiment concerning god particles or Higgs-Boson particles. It says that everything in this universe is waves and energy. In genesis, god expresses his wish and the world is created. Even in eastern religion similar myths are known. God wishes and the world came into existence. What was the guiding principle there? The answer is very obvious: "Desire". Desire is the guiding principle for the waves and the energy, for everything that exists in this universe. Human has the same power of desire.
Hence, you desire the answer and I am created."

He thought it must be some mysterious power which wanted to help him. He could not understand thc mysterious power completely but his intensive urge to know the secret made him speak with the power,
"I need some time to understand all these things. But now, I want to know answer of my question, what is the secret, the secret of life?"
The mysterious power,
"It is necessary to know what you consider as secret."
Am thought for a while and reply,
"I always wanted to know the meaningful way of living the life. I want to live every moment meaningfully. I don't want to die like stereotype animal. I did not mean I want to make death meaningful. I want to make my life meaningful. I do not know the meaning of "meaningful way" as well but I feel it very clearly."
The mysterious power,

"To live the life in our own desired way is the secret and this secret gives meaning to our life.

You are a social being. You are surrounded by various desires. In such situation it becomes necessary to understand what are our desired ways are. But there is a problem. Usually, human desires are guided by subconscious and impulses of unconscious. The past patterns and the proto-types control our Subconscious and unconscious. It could be a genetically received pattern. Hence, it is difficult to control desires. Consciously you want something but subconscious creates negation and your desire dies. But if your pattern supports your desire, you get it. You might have felt that we are puppets in the hands of our set past patterns.

It is partially true. One who learns or realizes the way to control his desires by creating new pattern, he knows the secret, the secret of life."

Am,

"I see! People, who knew the art, were recognized as great people, while others remained where they were. But I could not understand the concept of prototype."

The mysterious power,

"Prototypes are the basis for our perception, understanding, and action. Every human perceives the object through their five senses. These five senses perceives these object through basic prototypes or figures: square, round, triangle and their various combinations. Broadly the square represents the space in the universe. The triangle represents human's place in that space. While the round shape represents the cycle, movement. In other words, the change is

presented by the round shape. Human feels safe in motion. Ultimately, these prototypes are the boxes to carry waves and the energy.
Am,
"It means our prototypes controls and stores waves and energy. They are responsible for our way and status of life. Can we change our prototypes?"
The mysterious power,
"There are many suggested ways by various religions and thinkers. All are right in their own ways. By using our limited conscious we cannot come out of the influence of our prototypes which are set in our genes, subconscious and unconscious. These prototypes we receive from our great grand forefathers. It works through your subconscious. As you know 90 to 95 percent of activities are done subconsciously or unconsciously. You havc only five percent of scope to deal with your life.

Every living object is continuously engage in the process of creation since it is the law of the universe. The object which has stopped the process of creation is dead or dies. Hence, human being remains alive until the process of creation remains continue within him/her. Until hurdles are produced, human remains healthier. You need to understand the creation process:

The process of creation in human body or in any living object is same as the Big Bang, the beginning of universe. When two waves imbibing energy collide with each other with immense speed, the creation happens.

Human body follows the same process. It carries similar waves imbibing energy. These waves are traditionally known as soul. But these waves don't have enough speed for the creation process. Human body has a specific mechanism to increase the speed of the waves. It also requires the space for the collision. The same mechanism which increases speed and provide space for collision is known as chakras or energy centers. In fact, these centers are highly powerful accelerators which are responsible for the collision of the accelerated waves and the transmission of the created energy and the Higgs field at the specific area. There are in total seven chakras. The seventh chakra controls and balances other six chakras. Each chakra is responsible for the specific area of human body while the mental health depends upon the balance of all these chakras:

Root or Base Chakra:

Physical location of this chakra is base of spine. The area it governs is spinal column, kidneys, rectum, immune system, sexual organs of male and feet.

Sacral Chakra:

Physical location of this chakra is lower abdomen to the navel. The area it governs is sexual organs of female, liver, kidney, gallbladder, upper intestines, pancreas, adrenal glands, spleen and middle spine.

Solar Chakra:

The solar chakra is located below ribs. The area it governs is upper abdomen, umbilicus to rib cage, stomach.

Heart Chakra:

The heart chakra is situated at the center of the chest. The area it governs is heart, circulatory system, blood, diaphragm, breasts, esophagus, arms and hands.

Throat Chakra:

The throat chakra is located at throat and neck region. The area it governs is throat, thyroid, trachea, neck vertebrae, mouth, teeth, gums, parathyroid.

Brow Chakra:

It is located in the center of the forehead. The area it governs is brain, neurological system, eyes, ears, nose, pituitary and pineal glands.

Crown Chakra:

It is located at the top of the head. The area it governs is whole body and all psychological aspects.

Our accelerators control our body and mind. While these accelerators are controlled by our desires and our desires are controlled by our conscious, subconscious and patterns which we receive genetically and through social surroundings.

Have you asked yourself, "Why do you desire a change?" Because you are not satisfied with your life, you are not happy; things do not go as you want them to be, you believe you are lazy and impulsive, your life is not good enough, or something else. You must have tried various ways to change.

Am, you have read many books and experimented the ideas on yourself but you could not get satisfactory results. I will not include the things that you don't want. I will describe you the one of the most effective way to change your life. it will allow you to live life as per your desires. You will become free.

There is nothing magical in this exercise. It is not a religious process or anything that is fanciful. It is based on the laws of universe. I call this process "Mental Exercise". The exercise takes seven days to complete the first cycle. Every day you need to spend at least ninety minutes. If you discontinue in between, you have to reinitiate the exercise from the day one. For sixty minutes you cannot open your eyes. Keep your back straight as possible. You can change your position during the exercise. Now, listen the process carefully.

The seven days are divided in to three stages. Set an alarm for 60 minutes every day. Keep your body as straight as possible.

The first stage: (day 1 and day 2):

Step 1: Take your position. Close your eyes. Observe your body minutely as if you are travelling within you. Observe every part of your body objectively. Do not miss even a nail.

Step 2: When you feel that fifteen minutes are over, take a deep breath. Keep your eyes close. Now, you need to count your breathe up to 201 times. Do not try to control your breath. You simply need to count and experience your natural breath. If you are distracted by your imagination, thoughts or surrounding sound, you need to reinitiate counting from one. Try to focus on counting and experiencing the breath.

Don't worry if you cannot reach 201. Do the exercise for two days. This two days exercise prepares your body and mind for the change. It increases the capacity of the accelerators and it decreases the impulsive nature of your mind. You will feel your body lighter by third day.

Second Stage: (Day 3, Day 4, Day 5):

Step 1: Close your eyes. Repeat the step 1 approximately for five minutes and step 2 for ten minutes. You need to count your breath 51 times.
Step 2: Observe your complete body from top of your head. Now imagine you are releasing energy in your whole body till alarm rings. Just like earlier step, if you are distracted, do not worry. Focus on your task.
These three days will allow your seven accelerators to link with each other and prepares your body for the new pattern to develop.
Third Stage: (Day 6, Day 7):

Close your eyes and in your imagination, create a most important object or organism. After creating it, let the energy flow in your body. Your focus should be your creation during the process.

It is necessary to choose proper object or organism for the creation. The creation should remain with you till your death and you should be able to love it every moment.

Am, this exercise will enable you to live your life in your desired way. You will have your secret. Life is a flow. So, you need to get the answer of the proper object of the creation. Am, do not forget the symbol.

Am wanted to ask a question about the symbol that he experienced at the sea. But before he asked, the mysterious power asked Am to close his eyes and take a deep breath. He realized the mysterious sound was coming from within. He asked the mysterious power,
"Are you my inner voice?"
It replied,
"Yes, I am your creation."

Chapter: 10

The wind was flipping his diary. He looked at it. He looked for the mysterious sound but there was silence. He requested the mysterious power to talk with him but there was no response. He tried to search the innerself within. “Does it mean that he was talking to himself? He created all the mysterious experiences: the cosmic rhythm, the telephone talk, the grand figure and the secret.”, Am to himself.

He moved towards the hotel impulsively thinking over the question about the most important thing in his life, the fifth stage of the exercise. When he reached near the coconut tree, he saw two policemen searching something. Out of curiosity, he went towards them. They looked at him suspiciously as if he was a criminal. They questioned him why he was around in the dark night. Instead of answering their question, Am asked them whether he could help them or not. Am was surprised with his own behavior. He was unable to control his flow of words. They starred suspiciously at him. They could not understand Am’s intention. They did not like Am’s manner of the response.

They talked with each other in the local tongue. Am could not understand whatever they discussing. He told them the dog was buried there probably. They replied unconcerned,

“We are not worried about the dog but a serial murderer, not about the dog.”

Am,
"Yes, you can find two coconuts with the dog."

They became furious at Am. They shouted at Am to leave the place. Am could not understand why he was behaving like that. He recalled the words of the mysterious power. Let the desire flow freely. He decided to allow himself speak whatever the result would be. There must be some reason behind it which might be desired by the universe. He should keep faith in himself.

Am did not speak anything further. They thought he must be an insane fellow. But one of the police man observed Am closely. He said something to other policeman pointing towards Am. Both came near to Am. They asked him whether he knows anything about the serial murderer. Am denied. They asked him to describc thc morning incident and about him. Am thought the information about the morning incident might be useful to them. Am described,
"Yesterday night, I was on the shore. This dog came to me barking on something. It was afraid of something. It went back after sometime. When I came here, I saw the dog was dead. His head was full with blood. I lost my luggage in the police raid at the hotel that morning. It is with the police now. When I came back here, the coconut man with his son came here. They buried the dog with both the coconuts. And yes, there was dry blood stain on one of the coconuts. I think the dog might have died because of the coconut which might have fallen on him in the night.

Then, the coconut man asked me to follow him. I went to his home. I spent the whole day. Just before two hours I have come back. That's all."

Both were listening to him attentively as if Am was giving clues about the serial murderer. They asked Am the exact place where the dog was buried. Am recalled the morning incident. He recalled they put the dry leaves of the coconut tree on the grave. They dug it and took out both the coconuts. They took the blood sample which was on the head of the dog. One of the policemen came back to Am with two coconuts in his hands.

They ordered Am to stay there. Am was unable to understand their behavior. He asked hesitantly,

"Is there anything wrong?"

He unwillingly explained the truth,

"Sir, we suspect that whoever has killed the dog, he is the killer. We doubt that the man with whom you spent the whole day is the serial killer. If it is true, he will kill you tonight."

Am could not believe them. He gave reply,

"But the man lives with his son and he has already lost his family. He lives in hut. He sells coconuts. He comes here every day to pray the coconut tree. It is god for him. He is very kind fellow as well. He offered me meal and when I left his home, he gave me four coconuts as. I cannot trust you."

They again asked Am to stay near the coconut tree. They didn't want to take chance. They told him that he was very brutal. He had killed the visitors only. The police did not have much information about him. They asked him if he had seen any insane characteristic in him. Am was not sure about it. He thought for a while and replied,

"No, he is a simple man. He knows English. He told me that many visitors have taught him the language and he expressed gratitude towards them as well. I think he is a humble and innocent fellow."

One of them looked at Am. He asked Am about where the coconut man lived. Am showed them the way and explained the site. They telephoned through their satellite phone. In ten minutes one police van came. They were tensed. They went away towards the coconut man's house.

He was not sure whether the coconut man was the culprit or not, whether he gave wrong information to the police or not. After thinking for a while, he decided to note down the words of the mysterious power, especially the exercise. He opened his diary and wrote the exercise and the experiences at the sea. He thought his purpose to visit the place was accomplished. He would go back to his home tomorrow morning.

The police van came back after an hour. They asked Am to come near the van. He went there hesitantly. They were happy. One of them thanked Am. The other informed Am that they had caught the serial killer. Am inquired about the coconut man.

The police,

"Sir, you are lucky. You spent your whole day with him and you came back safe and alive. The coconut man is the serial killer."

Am was terrified. He could not utter a single word. He stood freeze. The police further explained,

"The coconut man has killed at least thirty visitors. He kept their luggage in his hut. We are surprised why you were spared. When we inquired about the reason for the murders, he became furious. Then, he described that he did not like the visitors because they do not understand the sea. They do not understand the Nature. They killed his family. They killed his coconut tree. And he killed all the visitors who stayed in the hotel where you were staying. After killing all the visitors of the hotel, he found your room empty. There was only some luggage. He took it with him. He locked all hotel staffs in one room. He used a big knife to kill the innocent visitors that he uses for cutting coconuts. He used the coconuts to kill the children. He is very brutal. Thanks again. If you need further help please fill free to contact us. Thank you very much for your information."

Am,

"What happened to the dog?"

The police,

"In the night, the coconut man climbed the tree and threw two coconuts on the ground. The dog was sleeping there. It became frighten. It must have come to you. But when it went back it was killed by the coconut man. He might not have liked its barking. The man killed three visitors in the night. Among them, there was a child of six years. His skull was broken probably with the coconut. We doubt he has used the same coconut which he used to kill the dog."

Chapter: 11

The whole picture became clear in the Am's mind. He thanked the policemen. Now, he understood the purpose of his inner voice. It wanted him to expose the killer. But he was unable to understand the relation between the incident and the secret. What he could learn through it. All perspective had changed. The coconut man had turned culprit from a hero. Is it about mystery of life? Or is it about the secret? He thanked the mysterious power for saving his life.

He looked above on the coconut tree. There were no coconuts. He recalled the belief of the coconut man. What might have happen to the boy?

One of the policemen,

"Sir, come here at the back door of the van and kindly check whether your luggage is here or not and everything is proper or not."

Am,

"How did you get it here? I think it was in your custody."

The police,

"Sir, we apologize for the inconvenience. In fact, we did not have your luggage. It was stolen. It was stolen by the serial killer. We found it just before twenty minutes."

Am found his luggage, checked his lap-top, credit cards, debit cards, and other possessions. Everything was proper. The police requested him to sit in the van. The police dropped him at the hotel. They described the hotel manager the whole incident. The hotel

manager was over whelmed. He greeted Am. The manager called up a staff, asked him to carry the luggage and put it in the luxurious room of the hotel. Before Am spoke, the manager continued,
"Sir, it is our pleasure to serve you. Your stay will be free of charge. Please, allow us to show our gratitude. Please sir, take rest. You must be exhausted. One servant will be always around you. Whatever you require, ask him. He will bring it in no time. For now, what would you like to have?"
Am,
"Thank you for giving me the honor. I don't need anything now. I am tired I need rest. And yes, accept my previous stay charges."
The manager,
"Sir, we can't take money from you. God don't allow us. You seem very tired. Please, get refreshed."

Am thought for a while and asked the manager, if he could arrange a vehicle in the morning. He wanted to visit the place of the coconut man early in the morning. He had to complete many unfinished tasks.
The manager was surprised. He asked Am,
"Sir, anything serious?"
Am looked at him. He observed the doubt, curiosity in the eyes of the manager. Am calmly,
"I am worried about the boy, the son of the coconut man."
The manager,
"Sir, you are a very nice human being. You worry about the boy of the killer. Your humanity touched us. We are really happy to help you. Do you need driver or would you like to drive yourself?"

Am,
"I will drive it myself."
Am wished him good night and went to the luxurious room. He took bath, changed his dirty cloths and asked the servant to bring a cup of coffee. He brought coffee along with some break-fast. Am thanked him. He ate it and drank coffee. He was happy and contended about his fate.

He slept in seconds. When he got up in the morning and the vehicle was ready. He took the diary with him. He drove towards the house of the coconut man. He was thinking about the boy. He reached there in ten minutes. He got down, walked towards the farm. He looked around, the hut was broken. He shouted for the boy. He did not know the name of the boy. There was no response. He went into the farm but there was no one. He looked up and he found there were no coconuts on any of the trees. He heard the sound of a goods carriage from the beach. He ran towards the sea. He saw the carriage. The boy was sitting behind. Am did not know the name. The boy recognized him. He asked the driver to stop the vehicle. The boy jumped down. The driver also got down. The truck was full with coconuts. The boy told Am in his own tongue that he has sold all coconuts to the big man. The big man translated it to Am. The boy was happy to see Am alive. But he did not know English. He could not express it in language but his expressions were clear. The big man told the whole story in detail:

When the police came here, this boy helped them to catch his father. His father was very cruel person. His father used to send him to beg on the beach. He was earning enough but he used to buy weapons to kill the visitors. So, for additional money, he forced the poor boy to work day and night. The boy liked you. He thought you must have been killed by his father. So, the police had come. But he seems happy to see you alive. He could not speak a word against his father. It is obvious. His father was sick, mentally sick. He lost his family due to the natural calamity but he thought that visitors do not understand the sea. They pollute it for their entertainment.

The boy interrupted the man. He wanted to say something. He told the big man to translate it in Am's tongue. The big man translated the boy's words:

"On the day of calamity, some visitors stayed in the hotel where you stay. They wanted to have coconuts. So, instead of purchasing it, they decided to cut the tree for the sake of their fun. They cut the tree. My father loved them much. We went there to collect the coconuts from the god tree. When my father saw the fallen tree, he became very sad. We came back home. My mother and all died in the same night. My father bought the weapons next morning. He killed all of them. But one ran away. Then after, he killed many visitors. But he liked you. He told me. My father liked you when he saw you playing with the sea waves. But he had doubt whether you really love the sea or not. I thought he killed you. I told police everything. They took him.

The boy climbed back the truck. The big man told Am that the boy would stay with him. He would help him in his work. He would live better life. Am wanted to help the boy. He put his hand in the pocket. He had around ninety bucks. He gave eighty five to the boy. The boy accepted the money hesitantly and gave a smile. The boy for the first time spoke in English, "Thank you". Both the boy and the big man went away.

Section: 3

Death of Kan

Chapter: 12

Am drove back to the hotel. When he went into the room, he heard a familiar sound. He recognized it was his mobile. He took it out from his pocket. He saw the sand wrapped on it. He thought it was dead. He cleaned the sand. He saw the screen was blinking. The mobile was working. The screen displayed an SMS. He opened it. The message was from some unknown number. The SMS:

"Am,

Kan is dead. Expect you to be here at home.

From: friend"

He could not trust the message. He immediately dialed back the received number. There was no response. He wanted to know the truth as early as possible. He was dropped to the air-port in nearby town by the hotel manager. Fortunately, he got the ticket.

In plane, he recalled how Kan had helped him, how they shared their lives. His eyes became wet. He began to sob. Am was very tensed. He slept in five minutes. He saw a dream:

'He was a boy of a ten or eleven year boy. He wore shirt and Bermuda. He was climbing a huge mountain. It was half dry, half green. It was steep. He was climbing on four legs. He saw some half dry grass, beside it there was a half black, half brown stone. It was difficult for him to climb it. But he was determined to climb. Gradually, he found it easy to climb the mountain. He could not see the end of the mountain. But he knew where he was going. After some time, he was growing faster. He was boy of sixteen year when he reached at the plane ground. He felt the growth normal. There was nothing surprising in it. Now, he wore informal cloths; jeans and t-shirt. There was water on the ground. He observed there were many people. They were trying to save themselves from the water. He felt there is nothing wrong with the water. It is safe. He was just about to put his foot in water; he saw hundreds of serpents in it. He observed them closely. They seemed harmless. Still he did not wanted to take risk.

He had to move ahead. So, he looked ahead. He jumped from one stone to another. Kan came to him. He told Am,

"Look! I have picked up many serpents. They are harmless. Do not worry. It is safe to walk in the water. They won't harm you."

Kan ran away happily. He disappeared in the smoke. People as well disappeared somewhere. He was alone. He decided to take risk. He put one foot in the water. It was warm water. He liked it. He put his second foot. The serpents raised their head towards Am. He became afraid. All serpents began to move towards him. He did not move. Suddenly, there appeared an old man wearing bright white cloths. He stretched his hands to help him. He instinctively gave his hand to the old man. When he reached near the old man who was half Kan and half coconut man, then he disappeared. And in surprise, there was no water, no serpents in next moment. He crossed the ground.

He reached at one corner of the garden. Many people were gathered there. All wanted to go into it.

But they were talking that there was no way to enter it. He found they must have some illusion. They can enter it from anywhere. It was a beautiful garden. He heard a man who was very much willing to enter it. He was describing the beauty of the garden. But he was not trying to enter it. It seemed that they were there for long time. He took first step. The way disappeared. There was a deep gulf before him. Beyond it there was a garden. He saw his parents in the crowd. They were unable to see him. He did not like to be with the crowd. He thought for a while. He recalled the third step of the mental exercise to let the energy flow in him.

He found himself away from the crowd. Now, he had to take decision whether he would keep faith in first vision or the second. He stepped ahead keeping faith in universe within. The gulf disappeared. He enter the garden. He looked towards the crowd. They were talking about him. All were surprised. He looked ahead. There was green lawn. He went in. Now, no one was visible. He was all alone. He saw one old book. There were some strange symbols on it. He was about to pick up the book, the book became half mobile and half book. The book received SMS. The sound of receiving SMS was very sharp. He could not bear it. The sound was becoming louder and louder. He stretched his right hand towards it. He was about to pick up the book..."

Am awoke. He was in the plane. He looked at his mobile. One SMS was open, "Are you sure?" it was an old SMS sent by Kan. He began to think about the dream. He began to connect his life with the dream. He understood his gradual development. He could not understand the old man in white attire who was half Kan and half coconut man. The gulf was representing his faith in the secret. The garden was representing his future life probably. The old book with symbol was presenting his diary in which he wrote all his experiences. The time melted quickly. He reached Kan's home after two hours journey.

Chapter: 13

Kan lived in a small flat with his wife and a son. He had only one small car. He was a professor. He could not afford luxury. When he reached the house, the door was opened by his father. He welcomed Am. He offered water to Am. The atmosphere at Kan's house was gloomy. His father sat near him and spoke in deep feeble voice,

"Son, Kan has went away. Before he left, he told me to give you something. Go in his room. It is there on the bed."

Am was horrified. He could not ask what happened to Kan. The various thoughts began to take shape in his mind. He recalled Kan's message,

"Kan is dead. Expect you to be here at home"

He walked slowly into Kan's room. There was a diary on the bed. On the front page of the diary there was the same symbol that he saw at the sea. He realized that the dream was about Kan's diary not about his diary.

He opened it. On the front page, Kan wrote,

"Kan,
My mind is like a naked woman
Who attracts desires of every sort,
But when I see you,
Her hands endeavor to become cloths
From: Kan"

Am thought,

"Kan must have written these lines to express his love towards himself which means he loves or loved himself very much. How artistically it is presented! He was genius. I could have helped him by sharing the secret of the universe, the secret of the life. My heart tells me that he is still alive. He can't go away like that."

He turned the pages of the diary. Kan had described his life, his struggles and his search for the truth behind it. He desired the secret, the secret of life. At the end of diary, he wrote that he was very near. Then on the last page, he wrote,

"Am,

Wherever we see there is a sea, vast and deep. We sail until our hope, not ship, sink in the abysmal.

From: the sea"

Am recalled the SMS which he received at the beach. He thought that Kan might have come to know about his end. He was very close to the secret of life. Now he himself has become a secret. He walked back to the room. He was sad. Kan's father asked him,

"Have you seen BMW M3 Miranda Red Devil E92 in the parking? He bought it few days back. Now, see! Nobody is here to drive it. I don't know driving."

Am did not know how to respond. Before he spoke anything the father asked him,

"Son, don't forget to see the Honda i-v new model, which Kan gifted to his wife. And wait till my grandson arrives. The driver has gone to pick him in Ferrari. Kan promised him to gift it to him and see! He has kept his promise."

Am was amazed by Kan's richness. He never gave importance to the money. But he always focused on the values of the better life.

Kan's father,
"Yes, Kan asked you to take a test drive of his BMW. He always added RED DEVIL after it. He never calls it a car. He used either BMW or Red Devil. But now, he is not there to enjoy the luxury."
Am looked down. He asked Kan's father to give the key of the Red Devil. He went down. He took a short drive and liked the BMW. He enjoyed the ride. When he came back, the Ferrari was there. It was a black Ferrari.

Kan used to talk about his desires. He often talked about the BMW. But Am never believed that Kan would ever have it. Am used to think that with such little earnings, Kan would never be able to have the BMW. Suddenly, a thought struck in his mind.
"Kan might know about the secret but if he knew it, he should not have died. But there is no confirmation of his death. He should know it. He could ask it to his son."

He went up. Kan's son and father were playing with each other. They asked Am to sit down comfortably. The son demanded chocolate from him. He forgot to but gift for the son in stress. Am apologized to him. The son played for half an hour and slept on the sofa. Am could not ask him about Kan's death.

Kan's father brought an album. He showed Am the photographs of Kan's childhood.
Kan's father,
"When he was child, I used to tell him about money crisis. But he taught me to think abundance of wealth. I often told him not to live in fancy. I forced him to see the reality around. Now, he is teaching the world a new

reality. He has proven that imagination is reality. Imagination is more real than everything else."

The father took some pause. He went into the kitchen and came out with a bowl. He put it on a hand of the sofa. It was full with the Cadbury Gems. He asked Am to have it. His father,

"He loves Gems. He often spoke about the Gems. He told me that he would have his own office. Instead of one side of the wall, he will keep glass. The water would run continuously run on them. And in such office, he will have tea. When someone would visit his office, he would offer them Gems which he would keep in big designer glass bowl. Now, he purchases four pound Gems every month. Please don't hesitate. I know we all love our childhood. Even I love."

Am,

"Kan never informed me about his progress. He shared everything but I could not understand why he hid it from me."

His father,

"Am, you are his best friend but you could not understand him properly. Even I could not. He lives in his own world which is more real than us'. I asked him to tell you about the progress. But he denied. He told me that Am will become unhappy because he is trying very hard to get the secret and till date he could not achieve the significance. But one day, he will find the secret and he will have everything."

"Now, it is confirmed that Kan knew the secret", Am thought.

Chapter: 14

His father went into Kan's bed room. He came out with an envelope. He sat near Am. Am sensed it was for him. His father kept the envelope with him and spoke,
"He once told me that when you would get the secret, you will visit our house. Have you got the secret?"
Am was amazed. He thought Kan knew everything about him. He knew I would visit his home after achieving the secret. Am wanted to say no but he could not. He nodded. The father,
"Kan asked me to ask you a question. The question is odd. Even I could not understand the significant of it. The question is, 'what is the difference between tea and coffee?' He has given me the answer. If you give me the correct answer I will be able to hand over this envelop to you. Take your time."

Am felt that he had become the part of some game. Now, he had the secret and still another secret was waiting for him. He thought for a while and tried to understand the answer from Kan's perspective. He recalled the mysterious power's words, 'life is a flow. You should find the most important thing of your life'.
Am answered instinctively,
"Both are waves and energy. The difference occurs when the desires get changed or restricted by our own older patterns and various prototypes."
The father,
"Do you know what answer he gave me? He said that he has faith in Am's ability. He will give the most

appropriate answer. He has not given me any answer. He asked me to understand the mystery of life. I asked him many time about his research but he never gave answer but this time when he left he told me that the answer of Am would be my research area."

Am,

"So, his research was about the waves and energy and prototype. He is amazing. He knew the secret from many years."

The father,

"Yes, he has been appointed as advisor in the grand project of World Innovation Organization. He has gone there for three months. He went just before a week. He is not allowed to use any communication means to contact out. The whole project is based on his idea. I could not understand his ideas, his flow of thinking."

The father giving him the envelop,

"Keep this. He said it would help you certainly. I have seen the pages. There are many symbols and strange language I could not understand it. Keep it."

Am became very happy to know that Kan is alive. It was a great relief. He inquired about Kan's wife.

The father,

"She will come late today. Every day she goes to teach painting. She is busy planning her first painting exhibition. She will be happy to see you here. Wait for her."

Am,

"Sure, I would like to have tea prepared by her. Kan loves tea. Kan loves to celebrate his success by drinking tea with friends. He is not here but I will celebrate his success by having tea at his home."

The father,
"You must be tired. Take rest in Kan's room. I will sleep with the kid."

Chapter: 15

Am observed the envelope. He was eager to know what was there in it. He went to the Kan's room. He opened the envelope and unfolded the papers. He wanted to go through the pages quickly. But when he saw the first page, he could not understand a single word:

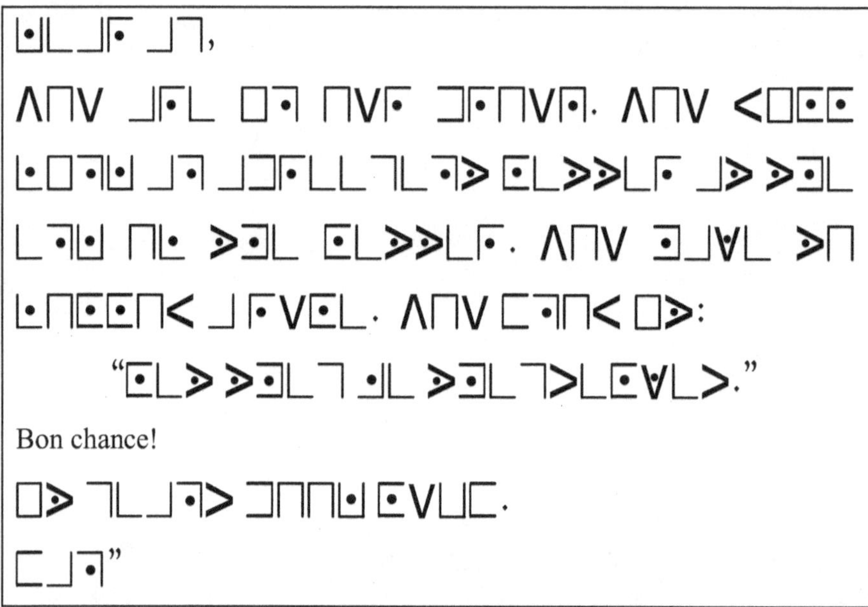

Bon chance!

There were some signs, dots as if it were a code language. He began to examine them minutely. But no use. He never saw such symbols. Only one word he thought it was in English, it was, 'Bon chance'. He realized even that phrase was not English. He recalled that Kan was learning French language. It must be French but the remaining part was mystery. He turned the page:

"Am,

I will teach you a new language, a new way to look at the world: the real world around us. When you came to know about the secret of life, you must have come across the prototypes: square, triangle, round and their various combinations."

Am recalled the mysterious power explained the prototypes but he did not find it very important. He did not take interest because he felt it was not his task to understand the secret of secret. He read further:

"First of all, learn the language. Observe the figure: 1 given below:

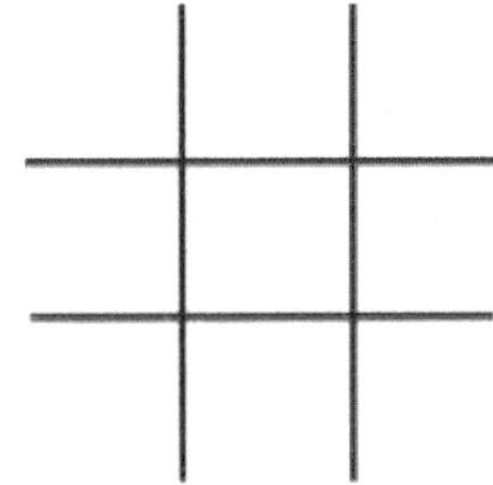

Now observe the figure 2:

Now, in your imagination, put each letter in each part. As it is given in the figure: 3,

ab	cd	ef
gh	ij	kl
mn	op	qr

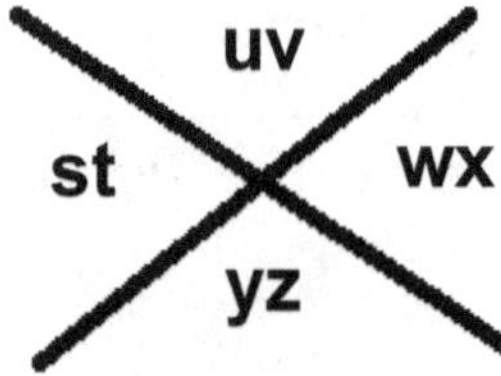

Separate each section in the given pattern:

┘ ⊔ └

⊐ □ ⊏

┐ ⊓ ┌

V

> <

Λ

Similarly, assign the symbol to each letter in the following way:

┘ = A	·┘ = B
⊔ = C	⊔· = D
└ = E	└· = F
⊐ = G	⊐· = H
□ = I	⊡ = J
⊏ = K	⊏· = L
┐ = M	·┐ = N
⊓ = O	⊓· = P
┌ = Q	┌· = R
> = S	>· = T
V = U	V· = V
< = W	<· = X
Λ = Y	Λ· = Z

And the numbers are ciphered in the following way:

··┘ = 1	⊔·· = 2	└·· = 3
⊐: = 4	□: = 5	⊏: = 6
··┐ = 7	⊓·· = 8	┌·· = 9
X = 0		

Hence, my name is written in this way:

Now try to write your name in the symbolic language.

It is so simple. Right? You have learnt a new symbolic language and the learning took only few minutes. There is an interesting myth about the prototype language. "If you write your wish in the square of the figure (given below as prototype design), the universe listen to you and grant your wish." And do you know the symbolical language refers back to the Freemason's Ciphers? We have made some changes to it. The Freemason's Ciphers was an effort to find the meaning of the figures. Fortunately, we could know the true significance of these figures and the use of them. I would like to describe you in brief the significance of the symbols:

The above figures show the prototypes. And these prototypes carry the waves and energy within them. Our senses send the information to our brain through the waves which are filled with energy. Our set pattern of prototypes in various combinations stores these waves. Then our subconscious began to function. It recreates the stored prototypes. It send the prototype to the accelerators. In this process, our feelings got attached to them. The speed of the waves is increased through the accelerators and our emotions and feelings. So, the prototype becomes unable to stabilize them and they began to move very fast. They move inside our body. Because of their immense speed, they wander in the every part of our body and they collide with each other and the process of creation starts.

If the waves are created with the similar intensity, the process of creation remains continues. And finally, the new matter is created or it brings the existing matter to the creator of the waves.

Hence, if we consciously accelerate our desires through the exercise that you have learnt and through our feelings, emotions, thoughts, it comes in our life or it is created. Obviously, it depends upon the intensity of our desire. Our intensity of continuous desire is the base of every creation whether we do it consciously or unconsciously. It is not about magical creation but we began to use our subconscious, unconscious and conscious simultaneously. We become more focused and we naturally began to enjoy the work that we do.

I have always tried to convey you the secret of the life but you did not want it from others. You wanted to have some mysterious experience. And I believe you have similar mysterious experience. The universe reflects only our desires. But don't forget the basics of prototypes. My research was based on the design of prototypes and how they affect our life. Especially, how we would be able to use them.

I have succeeded in my research. I want to share it with you. I have found some ways to use the prototypes. You can see the results. In six months, I could buy the BMW Red Devil, Ferrari for my son, Honda Accord for my wife and the continuous flow of money. Whatever I would need I have to use the prototypes.

When it comes to power, it should be controllable. So, before I tell you the way to fulfill the desire, I expect you to complete the agreement which is on the first page, written in cipher.

Am went back to the first page. He saw the letter. It was written symbolically. Now, he had learnt the way to decipher it. He understood the first phrase after deciphering every letter one by one. It was:

Dear Am,

Then Am wrote the letter in his diary. It was the same diary in which he wrote his experience of the mysterious power.

He deciphered:

Dear Am,

You are in our group. You will find an agreement letter at the end of letter. You have to follow 1 rule. You know it:

"Let them be themselves."

[Am could not understand the French word. He wrote the further deciphered words.]

It means Good Luck.

Am gave a smile. Now he understood the meaning of the French phrase. The last word was:

Kan.

Am realized Kan was playing a psychological game with him. He thought for a while and went back to the page where he left reading and read the note 'complete the first page'. He began to read further,

"I did not expect you to read from this page. I thought you would read the last page and see the agreement. But I am happy actually I am sure or may be not sure. Our absurd communication has always had

made some sense. I confess it has given me motivation to search further. I know I am not absurd as you always had thought. You might be thinking now that I am playing a game with you. Are you sure?
I know your answer, "I am not sure."

You have just learnt a new cipher. We search a lot years and finally we have got a design which helps us to control immense speed of our desires and the design help us to keep balance within us. The figure help us control the impulsiveness of our mind. If you imagine the figure while doing the exercise, you will be able to control your distractions more effectively. In short, it provides stability within. So, our continuous desires come really true. I experimented over the design and you know the results. The prototype design is given below:

The prototype design seems static but when you do the mental exercise, it begins to circulate with immense speed. It helps our accelerators or chakras to give additional speed to our desire and it also maintains the balance of all the accelerators and our body. In this way, it helps us to remain focused, overcome impulsiveness and achieve our desired goals.

We tried various religions' symbols. We analyzed their scriptures and various interpretations. We could not find the exact symbol but when we began to crosscheck them with basic prototypes, we began to get the clues. We succeeded in finding the design but the round figure was not making sense.

I focused on the meaning of these basic prototypes. Square means space, universe. Triangle means our place in the space or universe. While the round means the movement, change. It struck my mind suddenly. I understood the meaning of this indication. I realized that the static figure would be only visual illusion and when it began to move it becomes round. And we removed the round shape. The result is amazing.

Then I thought how the design could be helpful to us. I searched the books of every religion, symbols and quantum science. I found the exercise that you got at the sea. But the question of most important object was still a puzzle.

I decided to experiment on myself. I desired intensively the secret of creation, God within. For first three to four hours everything was normal. Suddenly, I experienced a blast within just like big-bang. My imagination began to take shape. I desired to create my own world. Initially, I found difficult to create because everything was unstructured. I desired beautiful creation. My imagination used my all energy. My soul, my mind, my body were got engaged in the process of creation. I choose most beautiful things from all the sources at hand.

I began to arrange everything in my world. It was my imagination which was playing the part of creator. My desires were guiding my imagination. I did not allow the things that I did not like. I focused on the creation. Do you know what I created? I created myself. I created Kan.

Am realized, he got the answer of the question asked by his inner voice at the sea about the most important object or organism of his life. It was himself.

After sometime, I felt the world that I was creating, was as real as outside world. I was very happy. It became difficult to control myself sometime. I began to forget the difference between the real world and the world I created within. The prototype design appeared in front of me. I calmed down. I came out of the inner world.

I completed the first cycle of the exercise. After some days, I began to get the things that I desired during creation of my inner world. I understood the importance of that experiment. Then, I kept the figure in front of me and again began to create a day for me. I kept away all those things and thoughts that I don't want.

Whatever I created in my world, I got all the things. Then I decided to prove it scientifically. Otherwise no one would believe me. On one day I met a person at coffee shop. I described him my creation and the design. He listened to me with interest. He was a scientist and member of 'World Innovation Organization'.

I received a letter from the scientist to become a part of the WIO (World Innovation Organization). We experimented the mysterious experience in various ways. Now, we have innovated some of the secrets of the universe.

In one of our experiments, we selected two thousand people of various regions. One thousand had better health and wealth while the others were from middle class families. We called them Group A and Group B. We asked them to create a most beautiful day of their life using their imagination. The only condition was that they should be able to feel their created world just like they feel dreaming in sleep. We used various tools to understand their mind, their waves, their level of energy, etc.

We come to know that Group A could imagine the real beautiful day of their own. While the Group B most of them found it difficult to create the day within.

After many researches, we have come to know that it is human's basic need to create something. Either we create consciously or unconsciously. When you create unconsciously, your creation is based on your past or your genetically received prototypes. If you create our world consciously, our past patterns also began to help us creating better world. But it is necessary to use the design to keep control over ourselves, our immense power within. The design has got approval from World Innovation Organization. Am, use the design, create your own world.

We will be able to meet each other only after three month. I will come to meet you at your house and we will have a cup of tea prepared by your wife."

The last words about the wife made Am nervous. He recalled how his wife left him before seven days. She told him that she would like to see him only in the court. He loved her much but he could never understand himself or her wife. He closed his eyes. He felt tears were flowing from it.

He knew what he should do now. He recalled pleasant memories that he shared and lived with his wife. He desired happiness and better relation with his wife. He desired it from bottom of his heart. Am turned the page. It was the agreement:

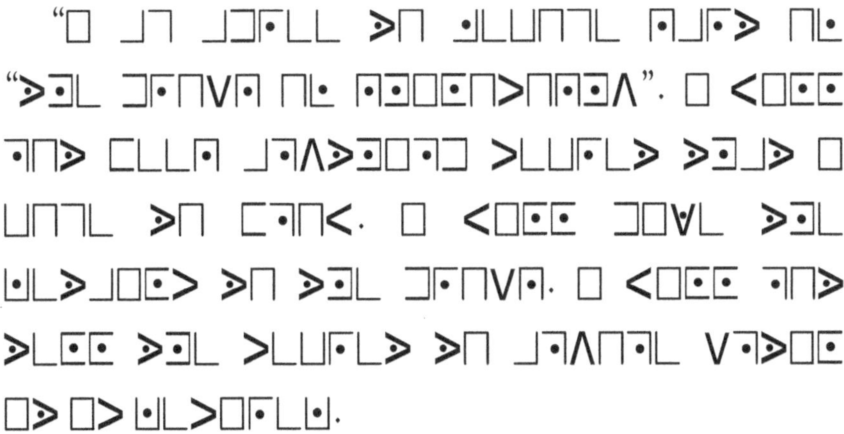

Am deciphered it. It means:
"I agree to become part of "the group of philosophy". I will not keep anything secret that I come to know. I will give the details to the group. I will not tell the secret to anyone until it is desired.

Signature"

Am signed the letter. He wanted to see the first letter. He turned back. All the pages were blank. Suddenly, he realized his mobile was ringing. It was an SMS. It was the same number from which he received the SMS about Kan's death. He opened it:

"Dear Am,

Thank u for joining the group. I hv faith in u and I know u   hv in me.
Kan"

Am could not understand how Kan knew about his signature. He looked up to find whether there are hidden cameras are kept or not. There was nothing which could be camera. The page began to shine. He saw them. Some words were appearing on them. He read:

"Am,

It is not miracle. The pages you held are not normal papers. They appear normal but they carry lakes of virtual particles. I can control them sitting here in the organization. Its only technology, it is not yet introduced in the market. They are under safety analysis. So that no one would be able to misuse them.

Kan..."

Am observed the page closely but he could not see any virtual particles. They were very normal pages. His mind was still occupied by the thought of his wife. He decided to do something immediately. He mobiled his wife. She did not pick it up. He tried many times but she did not give response.

Section: 4

The Myth of Life

Chapter: 16

He put back the pages in the envelope and came out of Kan's room. He hurriedly took leave from Kan's father. Kan's father could not understand his behavior and said

"Both (Kan and Am) are eccentric."

Am rushed to his wife's home. He received an SMS. He read:

> "Am,
> I want to talk to you. Can you meet me at 6 o'clock today in coffee house where you usually took me forcefully?
> Your Epuz"

Am was thrilled as if it was his first date. He reached the coffee house. He got out of the taxi. He replied:

> "Dear Epuz,
> I will reach there. I love you very much.
> Only yours"

He kept his mobile in his hand. He expected his wife's reply. There was no message for some time. The doubt about the meeting began to mount up. He asked himself to observe his internal desire. He began to think about their happy memories, their dreams. He thought he should gift her something valuable. He thought many things but he rejected all of them. He could not decide what to buy. Suddenly he recalled his college incident. Kan gave two leaves to a girl.

Am went into a nearby farm and took permission to take some leaves. He observed many trees, many leaves. He stopped near a tree. He searched the leaves on the earth. There were many dry leaves. He liked one leaf with two leaflets but he felt something was missing in it. He looked around. He liked trifoliate: a leaf with three leaflets. There were two yellow leaves and between them there was a small brownish red leave. He picked it up and went back to the coffee house.

On first instant, he wished to order a cup of tea but it was for the first time his wife asked him to have tea together. He decided to wait. He ordered French fries. He kept thinking about the meeting with wife.

Half hour was left. He received an SMS:

> "Am,
>
> I wanted to meet u in d coffee house but my health is not allowing me. Can we have tea at our house? I'm already there. Waiting 4 u."

After reading the SMS, he realized wife's positive indications. She is already at their house. She had forgiven him. He wanted to meet her immediately. But she had written about her poor health. He became worried. Many negative thoughts passed through his mind. He controlled his thoughts and expressed his desire to be happy family.

He replied:

> "Dear Epuz,
>
> Not a problem. I'll reach there. On the way.
>
> Take care
>
> Your Am"

He got up, paid the bill and looked around for taxi. He got one. He looked out of the window. It was his home town. He was happy to see the roads, buildings, the monuments and the people as if he had come back there after years. He realized it was the beginning of his new life. He loved the busy roads. It was full of life unlike the sea town.

He saw a gift article shop. Impulsively, he asked the driver to stop the taxi. He wanted to make the leaf trifoliate precious. He decided to buy some archaic box for the leaves. He went through many boxes. He liked a box on which the image of Shiva, God whose image helped scientist to understand the Higgs Boson particles, was carved on it. He put the trifoliate into the box. The shop keeper offered to gift pack it. But he did not like to get it packed. He wanted to keep it open. He did not want to wrap the beautiful things. He wanted to show the leaves as early as possible to his wife. He wanted to express his love, his in-depth feeling through the leaves.

He got into the taxi. He kept the box in his hand. Before he reached home, he received an SMS:

"I wanted to give you the news. I can't wait more. I left our home, reached my parents' home, contemplated for three days and realized u love me lot. You must be passing through difficult period. I should have been with you instead of running away. I should have supported u. I know u will forgive me. I got ready to come back to home suddenly I fainted. I went to the doctor. He gave me the great news. We will be three now. You dreamed since long. Now, it has come true.

Congratulations!!!

Yours Epuz"

He reached home in fifteen minutes. He jumped out of the taxi. He had paid in advance for the taxi. He was over joyed. He rushed into the home.

Chapter: 17

After four days:
Am had been doing the exercise which was suggested by the mysterious power or might be his inner voice for last four days. In his office, Am was more confident. He thought everything would change suddenly just like Kan. With the exercise and he often used the prototype design of Kan. He was very happy. He would become father soon.

After a week:
Am completed the first cycle of the exercise. Initially, he could not imagine himself in the process of creation but on the seventh day he succeeded. He realized the world he created was not real as it was explained by Kan. He was eagerly waiting for the change in his life.

After two months:
Am again began to struggle in his routine life. He could not live with confidence that he experienced at the sea. Again the negative thoughts began to mount around him. He decided to continue with the Exercise. He usually told himself that Kan did it and he was a successful and happy person. So, he could be. He kept the diary with him while he meditated.

He went with his wife for the routine checkup. Both came back tensed. The doctor informed them that the child growth was very slow. So, they should be mentally prepared for uncertainty. Am supported his wife much. He left the part time job. He spent more time with his wife. The incident did not affect his faith in mysterious power and Kan. But he left doing the exercise regularly.

After two years:

Am was a successful businessman. He left the full-time job thirteen months back and tried his luck in business. He lost heavily in the first venture. His wife supported him to start a new business. He fortunately got success and now he has all the luxury. He owns his dream cars, house and the big statue of Shiva. He had sixteen months child. His wife was happy.

He gradually realized that there is nothing like secret in life. It is about our approach towards the life. He stopped doing the exercise before six months. He kept his diary somewhere in his personal library.

Chapter: 18

Am was drinking coffee in the balcony of his new bungalow in the half-moon night. He received an SMS. It was Kan's:

> "Read email. It's important."

Am opened the email in his virtual tablet:

> "Dear Am,
> I have attached your emails that you sent me before two years. If find time, read them.
> Kan"

Am read those emails after few hours. The visit to the mysterious sea coast began to float in Am's mind. He received an SMS just that moment:

> "Am,
> Is there any secret of life?
> Can"

Am went out in the open sky. It was starry night. He smiled. He gave reply to Kan:

> "Dear Kan,
> I will send you my experiences to you. But I will take two to three days to write everything. I need to cover two years in it. I have not forgotten the agreement.
> Thanxs
> Am"

www.ingramcontent.com/pod-product-compliance
Lightning Source LLC
LaVergne TN
LVHW091557170726
843492LV00007B/2169

* 9 7 8 8 1 9 2 1 3 1 1 2 2 *